Cooking for Mr. Right

Add a little spice
to your life!
Mimi Bean

Cooking for Mr. Right

Mimi Bean

with Rebecca Chastenet de Géry

CITADEL PRESS
Kensington Publishing Corp.
www.kensingtonbooks.com

CITADEL PRESS BOOKS are published by

Kensington Publishing Corp.
850 Third Avenue
New York, NY 10022

All Kensington titles, imprints, and distributed lines are available at special quantity
discounts for bulk purchases for sales promotions, premiums,
fund-raising, educational, or institutional use. Special book excerpts or
customized printings can also be created to fit specific needs. For details, write or
phone the office of the Kensington special sales manager: Kensington Publishing
Corp., 850 Third Avenue, New York, NY 10022,
attn: Special Sales Department; phone 1-800-221-2647.

CITADEL PRESS and the Citadel logo are Reg. U.S. Pat. & TM Off.

First printing: March 2006

10 9 8 7 6 5 4 3 2 1

Printed in the United States of America

Library of Congress Control Number: 2005934015

ISBN 0-8065-2702-1

I dedicate *Cooking for Mr. Right* to my father,
William Riley Bean, II,
The Original Grill Master
Who made me his kitchen sidekick as a child,
and made the best hush puppies
I ever put in my mouth!

Contents

Part 2: In the Mood

Introduction

Let's face it. At some time or another, snagging a man is on almost every girl's—and the occasional boy's—mind. And the old adage rings true: There's no better path for sending that arrow flying straight to a man's heart than through his stomach. That's why we've written *Cooking for Mr. Right*. With it, you and your dish will always be cooking!

The following pages deliver the goods you need to get the man you want. Each menu is straightforward, festive, and easy, and its recipes and techniques foolproof. Plus, our atmosphere-enhancing tips and side-bars go the extra mile in helping you capture the ideal mate. The menus that follow are brand new—tailor-made for your man and every occasion you may face.

Don't feel like cooking? No problem. This scintillating cookbook still makes for great bedside reading. Tuck yourself in with it, and rest assured that you've found *the* "how to" manual to have on hand when you want to nourish a man's soul, feed his many appetites, and fuel his libido. Sly, witty, and positively tempting, the recipes that follow will find you tying on that apron and donning your kitchen goddess hat in no time.

Got it in for the Rugged Outdoorsman? Speak to his natural instincts with Hot Bacon Spinach Salad, Roasted Wild Duck, and Georgia Peach Pie. Seducing a Starving Artist? Satisfy his creative impulses with Curried Peanut Chicken, Hunan Pork Dumplings, Zesty Zucchini, and a funky little Floating Island for dessert. Aiming to impress a dashing Daddy Warbucks? Make your Grill Master's heart race with Grilled Porterhouse Steaks. And rely on the book's clever music pairings to spice up Mr. Right's menu with tunes that will have your and his fingers dancing before the dishes have even been cleared.

In the spirit of "you are what you eat," *Cooking for Mr. Right* also helps you cook for the occasion. The second part of the book is dedicated to taking culinary advantage of your situation, and makes sure you get the mood right for love no matter what type of man you've brought home. There's a menu aimed at Pure Seduction, featuring Corn Blinis with Crème Fraîche and Caviar, Salmon Wellington, and Chocolate Truffles. A lesson on Aphrodisiacs 101 with tastes like Scallops Ceviche, Oysters on the Half Shell with Pink Peppercorn Mignonnette, Fried Lobster Fingers with Honey-Dijon Sauce, and Champagne Sorbet. There's even a delicious formula for easing into The Morning After. And when it's time to say good-bye and move on to your new man, nothing makes the transition easier than the book's Dear John Dinner of Chilled Cucumber Soup, Cold Chinese Noodles, and Lemon Ice.

For those whose dreamboats seduce from the spotlight,

Cooking for Mr. Right goes where no cookbook has ever gone before. The book's third part is chock full of the dream menus of some of the world's most desirable men—TV and movie stars, playboys, authors, and chefs. These are the guys everyone wants to snare, and now their secrets for seduction are out in the open! Even if you can't get your hands on these guys, their ideas about foods that tempt and tantalize just might translate into an unforgettable evening with a man who is within your reach.

Turn up the heat, and get that seduction game going. You'll soon find that the pantry and fridge hold almost all the necessary temptations to get your man's mouth watering. Then follow our foolproof steps, season with a little bit of you, and you'll give Mr. Right exactly what he's craving.

Acknowledgments

Cooking for Mr. Right would not be in your hands right now if I had not received such strong support and inspiration from the many people who have helped to shape my culinary life. It all began at age five, when my family spent time at a lake house on Lake Burton in the North Georgia Mountains. I took to fishing right away, and spent countless hours, pole in hand, casting from our boat dock. Every day, I ran back to the house with a string loaded with little lake brim. It didn't take long before my grandmother, Elsie, said, "Honey, if you're going to catch these fish, you need to learn how to clean them so you can eat them. We're not going to have a bunch of smelly dead fish brought to the house every day." So at five, I was cleaning fish with her. I think this was the crucial moment that freed me from any sort of intimidation in the kitchen. From that day on, I have been able to handle food products with ease. I know many adults who are afraid to handle raw meat and seafood. I guess my willingness to roll up my sleeves and dive right in means that my friends often have a better time at dinner at my house than at their own.

This book has been in the making for ten years and there are plenty of acknowledgments I need to make. My childhood friend Kelly Sweetin coined the phrase "snag-a-man meals" when I was secretly making dinners for her then boyfriend, now husband, Greg. He loved what I prepared behind the scenes in Kelly's cookware, playing the Cyrano de Bergerac of her kitchen. By the way, she is an excellent cook!

Thanks to my dad for waking me up early in the morning to make weekend breakfasts with him. His favorite? Toll House Eggs. And thanks, too, to my mom, Geri Bean. Dinner was always a team effort in her kitchen. She delegated well and we learned to cook, getting it all to the table for dinner as a family every night. Thankfully, I got to make the sauces—a job that helped fine-tune my palate early on.

Dear friends who have shaped my skills are Lynne and Howard Halpern, Amy Fisher, Barbara Zeeman, my brother Bob Bean, who cooked with me as a kid, and my sister Tricia Schachtel, who turned me on to the idea of cooking schools. She went to Ursula's in Atlanta, impressing me with her baking skills while I was still in high school. To my girlfriends who have entertained with me and played in the kitchen over lots of laughs and wine: Donna Marshall, Carol McFarlane, Diana Brinson, and Cappy McAlpin. Carol was the first person who really taught me how to throw a dinner party! The one person I wish could see this book is Judy Falk. I adored her, her love of food, and her passion for detail. She changed my desires for the better, and I miss being able to discuss cooking ideas with her.

Finally, a big thank-you to the team that put this all together. Mae Rainwater pushed me along by introducing me to my co-author, Rebecca Chastenet de Géry. Claire Landiss introduced me to my literary agent, Karen Gantz Zahler, and Carolyn O'Neil provided neverending help when I didn't know the next step.

Last but not least, here's to the men in my life who have appreciated my passion. To George Lefont, who sent me to France to work with culinary wizard Roland Mazere. To Guy Cihi for his lifelong friendship and love of Bordeaux wine. The man I refer to as "the Melon Man" for his organic delicacies, passion for life, good taste and excellent palate. To my new friend Seth, whom I refer to as "Stealth," who has a natural love and passion for food, friends, and *joie de vivre*. We love talking about ingredients and technique. I have had many great dinner parties with the help of Andrew Sugrue. He can always read my mind in the kitchen with no stress. And to Lucky Luca, who has given me daily love and support while writing this book from Costa Rica, which has been a rich place for me to live for the past year.

Cooking for Mr. Right

part 1

Wooing Mr. Right

He's your kind of man from head to toe –
the domineering Alpha Male, the sweet Mama's Boy,
the merry Grill Master, the worldly Magnate. Whatever
your type, ply him with foods that speak to his soul,
dishes that satisfy his innermost cravings. When the
menu's and meal's atmosphere speak straight to "Mr.
Right," he'll be eating out of your hands by dinner's
end! This chapter is all about catering to your man—to
unlocking his heart by way of his stomach. Satisfy his
ego—you took the time to notice the "real" him—and
you'll snag him for sure.

In the following pages, you'll find multi-course
menus specifically created to speak to the appetites of
dozens of different types of men. Go on! Give him a little
taste of paradise. There's protein-packed Steak Tartare
for your domineering Alpha Male, a red wine–soaked
Coq au Vin for your hip Euro-Nerd, Soufflé Grand
Marnier to impress the discriminating Mr. Magnate,
and plenty of meat on the bone to appease Mr. Big,
Bad, and Rippled. In addition to the thoughtfully and

intentionally selected appetizers, entrées, and desserts, each menu features a song to start your evening off on the right note. Heed our wine or beverage pairing suggestions, and you'll up your seduction ante for sure. Our expressly selected wines, spirits, and elixirs will get Mr. Right's juices flowing!

Half of the seduction game is getting the mood right, so be sure to take a close look at our Setting the Stage chart at the end of this chapter. It outlines a handful of simple atmosphere-enhancing steps you can take to insure you're getting the mood ripe for love. Break out those batik print table linens for your Eternal Peace Corps officer. Make your Mama's Boy feel at home with fresh fingertip towels and a flickering votive in the bathroom. Set your table the French way for Mr. Euro-Nerd. And get the foolproof secrets for effortlessly starting a roaring fire in front of your Rugged Outdoorsman.

Dinner not in your plans? We've still got the recipe you need to snag that man. Woo Mr. Right over with drinks at your place by relying on our Cunning Concoctions chart. It features easy-to-assemble nibbles designed to jump-start your date and complementary cocktails chosen specifically with your man in mind. Or concentrate your efforts on a late-night rendezvous. Rely on our After Hours food and drink pairings to create an amorous atmosphere in the wee hours.

Finally, remember to keep things loose and sexy. Want to snag an Alpha Male who just can't stay away from the grill or a Music Man with plenty of Euro-Nerd sensibilities? Mix and match the recipes in our menus to best suit your multi-faceted man. One bite, and he'll come running back for more.

Chapter 1
The Alpha Male

He's self-assured and in control; the strong, silent type or the outspoken life of the party. Regardless, your Alpha Male wears the pants all the time. Cater to his dominance with plenty of raw protein, a feisty touch of spice, and a bright, bracing finish. This menu presents the ultimate Surf & Turf for the power-hungry man. The protein-packed Steak Tartare will fuel your Alpha male's desire to dominate, while the sweet, soft, Savannah Lump Crab Cakes with their luscious Red Remoulade Sauce will soften any of his brash edges (not to mention keep his mind on you). A hint of voluptuous cream mingles suggestively with the supremely macho side dish of Wild Mushrooms En Croute. And when dessert exits the kitchen, your Alpha Male will appreciate that you haven't gone all soft and sweet on him. A tart, spirited Key West Key Lime Pie finishes the meal on an appropriately bold, bright, energizing note.

THE SONG: *Under My Thumb* by The Rolling Stones

THE WINE: Grigich Hills California Chardonnay

Steak Tartare with Toast Points

A LITTLE MEAT GOES A LONG WAY IN THIS CLASSIC FRENCH APHRODISIAC INVIGORATED BY LIVELY GARLIC, EARTHY ANCHOVY, AND THE LIBIDO-ENHANCING LUSTER OF A FRESH, RAW EGG. FOR ALL OF ITS "UP FRONT" PROTEIN, STEAK TARTARE IS SURPRISINGLY LIGHT FARE THAT WON'T WEIGH YOU OR YOUR MAN DOWN.

½ pound prime beef tenderloin, ground through a medium blade immediately prior to serving (see Note)
1 teaspoon garlic, chopped fine
1 tablespoon capers, chopped fine
1 tablespoon anchovies, chopped fine
1 fresh egg yolk
1 tablespoon Dijon mustard
1 tablespoon extra-virgin olive oil
1 teaspoon cracked black pepper
Dash of Tabasco
Juice of half a lemon
Salad leaves for presentation
Chives for garnish
French bread, sliced into ¼-inch-thick rounds and toasted

Combine the ground tenderloin, garlic, capers, anchovies, egg yolk, mustard, olive oil, pepper, Tabasco, and lemon in a large mixing bowl, using your clean hands to blend the mixture gently until the seasonings are well incorporated into the meat. Divide the tartare into two 4-ounce patties. Or if you prefer, form the tartare into one large patty. Using a knife, make "grill"-type marks on the patties. Line a platter with fresh salad leaves, add the meat patties to the plate, and sprinkle them with fresh chives. Serve with toasted French bread.

MAKES 2 SERVINGS.

Note: If you don't have a meat grinder at home, purchase the tenderloin just prior to the meal and ask your butcher to grind the meat for you. Do not use pre-ground, packaged hamburger meat.

Savannah Lump Crab Cakes with Red Remoulade Sauce

CITIES DON'T COME SEXIER THAN SAVANNAH, WITH ITS STEAMY, MOSS-LADEN, PLANTATION ATMOSPHERE INCITING RHETT BUTLER–STYLE ROMANCE. AND CRAB CAKES—A SAVANNAH SPECIALTY—DON'T COME TASTIER THAN THESE LUMP CRABMEAT MOUNDS. DON'T SCRIMP ON THE CRABMEAT. GOOD CRAB CAKES KEEP THE EMPHASIS ON CRAB AND DISPLAY A LIGHT TOUCH WHEN IT COMES TO THE BREAD AND CRACKER CRUMB FILLING.

½ pound jumbo lump crabmeat
1 tablespoon lemon juice
½ teaspoon dry mustard
1 medium egg
1 sprig fresh thyme leaves, chopped fine
1½ tablespoons fresh chives, chopped
1 tablespoon fresh parsley, chopped fine
1 teaspoon Worcestershire sauce
Pinch of ground cayenne pepper
1 teaspoon Old Bay seasoning
¼ cup mayonnaise (preferably Hellmann's)
3 tablespoons cracker crumbs (preferably Saltines)
½ cup bread crumbs
2 ounces butter
1 tablespoon olive oil
Salt
Freshly ground black pepper
Lemon wedges to garnish

Pick over the crabmeat, removing all shells and cartilage. Set aside. In a large bowl, mix the lemon juice and dry mustard together until they form a smooth paste. Add the egg, thyme, chives, parsley, Worcestershire sauce, cayenne, Old Bay seasoning, mayonnaise, and cracker crumbs and mix well. Gently fold the crabmeat into the mixture, taking care to break up the meat as little as possible. Form the mixture into small cakes and coat each one lightly with bread crumbs. Chill for one hour. In a heavy skillet, heat butter and olive oil and fry the crab cakes 2 to 3 minutes on each side until they are golden brown. Season with salt and pepper to taste. Drain the crabcakes on a paper towel and keep them warm until ready to serve. Serve with Red Remoulade Sauce and garnish with lemon wedges and parsley sprigs.

MAKES 2-4 SERVINGS.

Red Remoulade Sauce

THE SOUTHERN WAY TO LIGHT A FIRE UNDER ORDINARY MAYONNAISE, REMOULADE SAUCE ADDS A FEISTY KICK TO SOFT, COMFORTING LUMP CRAB CAKES. DOUBLE THE RECIPE IF YOU WISH. REMOULADE ELEVATES ORDINARY CRUDITÉS AND STANDARD SANDWICHES TO GOURMET STANDING.

1 sweet red bell pepper, seeds and ribs removed, roasted and peeled
1 cup mayonnaise (preferably Hellmann's)
1 scallion, minced
Zest of 1 lemon, minced
¼ cup fresh dill, chopped fine
1 tablespoon freshly grated horseradish
1 tablespoon capers, rinsed, drained, and chopped fine
¼ cup parsley, chopped

Puree the roasted red bell pepper with the mayonnaise in a food processor or blender until smooth. Add the remaining ingredients and continue to puree until smooth. Transfer to a serving bowl and chill for at least 30 minutes prior to serving.

Wild Mushrooms en Croute

NO "PANSY" VEGETABLE MEDLEY FOR THE ALPHA MAN. FEED HIS EGO INSTEAD WITH THESE ÜBER MASCULINE FRUITS OF THE EARTH. MUSHROOMS ARE SUPREMELY RUSTIC AND UNDENIABLY MALE. THE STRONG FLAVOR FOUND IN THIS QUARTET OF WILD FUNGI DOMINATES DESPITE A GENEROUS DOSE OF TAMING CREAM AND A LIGHT, PASTRY TOPPING. THIS IS A BOLD, GENTLEMANLY, STEAKHOUSE-TYPE "SIDE" AT ITS FINEST.

3 large shallots, chopped fine
1 tablespoon olive oil
4 ounces Shiitake mushrooms, sliced
4 ounces oyster mushrooms, sliced
4 ounces chanterelle mushrooms, sliced
1 pound button mushrooms, sliced
1 cup white wine
4 cups beef stock (two 16-ounce cans beef broth)
4 cups heavy cream
2 tablespoons Worcestershire sauce
2 teaspoons salt
1 teaspoon white pepper
2 tablespoons sugar
4 ounces cornstarch, dissolved in cool water
Puff pastry sheets

Preheat the oven to 375 degrees F. Heat the olive oil in a large skillet and add the shallots, sautéing over high heat until translucent. Add the mushrooms and continue sautéing over high heat until the mushrooms have softened. Add the white wine, beef stock, heavy cream, Worcestershire sauce, salt, white pepper, and sugar and bring to a boil. Add the dissolved cornstarch and continue stirring until thickened. Remove the mushrooms from heat and allow them to cool, tasting to check the seasonings. Transfer the mushrooms to an ovenproof bowl, filling it to 1/4-inch from the top. Cover the bowl with the puff pastry and seal it tightly around the edges. Bake at 375 degrees for 12 minutes.

MAKES 6-8 SERVINGS.

Note: Puff pastry sheets are generally found in the frozen food section of your local supermarket.

Key West Key Lime Pie

THIS SCINTILLATING DESSERT TEASES THE PALATE WITH ALTERNATING SWEET AND TART NOTES, AND CLOSES DINNER WITH A PREVAILING ATMOSPHERE OF HIGH-SPIRITED SEDUCTION—A MOOD PERFECTLY SUITED TO THE ALPHA MALE.

1 tablespoon unflavored gelatin
1/2 cup sugar
1/4 teaspoon salt
4 egg yolks
1/2 cup Key lime juice (see Note)
1/4 cup water
1 teaspoon grated lime zest
Drop or two of green food coloring (optional)
4 egg whites
1 cup heavy cream, whipped
1 baked 9-inch pie shell, cooled, or 1 9-inch graham cracker pie shell
Additional grated lime zest for garnish
1 tablespoon shelled pistachios to garnish

Mix the gelatin, sugar, and salt thoroughly in a saucepan. In a separate bowl, beat together the egg yolks, Key lime juice, and water. Add the egg mixture to the gelatin mixture and cook over medium heat, stirring constantly, until the mixture comes to a boil. Remove from heat immediately and stir in the lime zest. Add food coloring (optional) sparingly to give the mixture a pale green color. Chill, stirring occasionally, until the mixture mounds slightly when dropped from a spoon. Beat the egg whites until soft peaks form and gradually add the 1/2 cup sugar, beat until stiff peaks form. Smooth the chilled lime mixture into the pie shell and top with the whipped cream.

Chill until firm. Just prior to serving, add additional whipped cream to the pie's topping and edge the pie with grated lime zest. Top with grated pistachios in the center, bordered by thin half-circles of lime.

MAKES 6-8 SERVINGS.

Note: If Key limes are not available, substitute Joe's Key Lime Juice, a bottled lime juice product widely available in supermarkets and liquor stores.

Chapter 2
Big, Bad, and Rippled

You can't get enough of his thick, sinewy arms; his taut, broad chest; and his six-pack abs. Keep your hunk's well-tuned engine running with a man-sized meal of Herculean proportions. Pump him up with hearty Brunswick Stew—iron-fortified BBQ in a bowl. Then continue the man-style meal with a rack of Baby Back Pork Ribs as hot and rippled as his own. The Cayenne-Chili Rub that dresses the ribs is sure to get his pulse racing. Cool him down just a wee bit with Fresh Blackberry Pie, a fresh-fruit treat more invigorating than any supplement your muscle-bound Adonis may normally pop. Come meal's end, Mr. Big, Bad, and Rippled will have softened to putty in your hands. Climb aboard and ride his waves.

THE SONG: *You'll Accomp'ny Me* by Bob Seger

THE BEVERAGE: Miller Genuine Draft, 5 longnecks in an iced bucket

Brunswick Stew

SOUTHERNERS LOVE TO ARGUE OVER BRUNSWICK STEW'S ORIGINS. WHETHER THIS HEARTY CURE FOR ANYTHING-THAT-AILS-YOU WAS FIRST STIRRED IN VIRGINIA, SOUTH CAROLINA, OR GEORGIA, NO MATTER, MR. BIG, BAD, AND RIPPLED CAN SOLVE THE DISPUTE. REGARDLESS OF ITS HERITAGE, BRUNSWICK STEW'S DOUBLE-MEAT AND MASHED POTATOES BASE WILL HAVE YOUR BULGING MAN STRUTTING HIS STUFF AS PROUDLY AS ANY MR. UNIVERSE.

2 tablespoons vegetable oil
1 medium onion, chopped
1 green bell pepper, diced
2 pounds cooked chicken, cut into 1/2-inch pieces
1 10-ounce can Castleberry's brand BBQ pork
3 cups water
2 14-ounce cans chopped tomatoes, not drained
1 tablespoon Worcestershire sauce
1 teaspoon Tabasco
2 tablespoons parsley, chopped
2 cups corn
2 cups lima beans
2 potatoes, peeled and diced into 1/2-inch cubes
1/2 cup Kraft's Hickory Smoked BBQ sauce
Salt
Ground black pepper
1/4 cup cider vinegar
1 teaspoon paprika

Heat the vegetable oil in a pot large enough to hold the stew, and add the onion and pepper, sautéing until translucent. Add the chicken, BBQ pork, water, tomatoes with their liquid, Worcestershire sauce, Tabasco, and parsley and bring to a boil. Reduce heat, cover, and simmer for 15 minutes. Add the corn and lima beans and cook for 20 minutes longer. Meanwhile, cook the potatoes until tender in water and put through a food mill or ricer to mash. Add the mashed potatoes to the pot and stir. Add BBQ sauce, salt, pepper, vinegar, and paprika and serve.

MAKES 6 SERVINGS.

Baby Back Barbeque Ribs with Cayenne Chili Rub

THIS SLAB OF LIP-SMACKIN' RIBS IS FINGER FOOD FIT FOR A MEATY MAN. THE RACK'S DRY CHILI RUB INFUSES THE PORK WITH THE KIND OF "HURTS SO GOOD" SLOW-BURN MR. BIG, BAD, AND RIPPLED APPRECIATES. DON'T BE INTIMIDATED BY THE RECIPE'S LONG LIST OF INGREDIENTS. THE RIBS COME TOGETHER IN FOUR EASY STEPS—RUBBING, ROASTING, BASTING, AND GRILLING.

1½ slabs baby back ribs, skin removed
3 tablespoons cider vinegar
Heavy-duty aluminum foil

FOR THE CAYENNE CHILI RUB:
3 tablespoons chili powder
3 tablespoons ground black pepper
3 tablespoons paprika
2 tablespoons garlic powder
2 teaspoons cayenne pepper
1 tablespoon salt
2 tablespoons onion powder

FOR THE BASTING SAUCE:
1 clove garlic, crushed
⅓ cup firmly packed brown sugar
2 tablespoons olive oil
½ cup catsup
2 tablespoons Worcestershire sauce
1 tablespoon prepared yellow mustard
2 tablespoons red wine vinegar
¾ teaspoon chili powder
1 teaspoon black pepper
½ teaspoon hot pepper sauce

Preheat the oven to 250 degrees F. Wash and dry the ribs. You should have three sections of approximately eight ribs each. Prepare the Cayenne Chili rub by mixing all the ingredients in a small bowl until well blended. Once the ribs have dried, coat the front and back of each rack generously with the Cayenne Chili rub. Cut three sections of heavy-duty aluminum foil large enough to wrap each rack of ribs entirely. Place the seasoned rib sections in the foil and gently pour one tablespoon of cider vinegar into each foil pack and seal tightly. Place the packs on a large cookie sheet and cook in the preheated oven for two hours.

Prepare the basting sauce by mixing all the ingredients together in a medium saucepan. Warm over medium heat for 10 minutes, stirring frequently, and set aside.

Once the ribs have been removed from the oven, grill them over medium heat for approximately 10 minutes, continuously brushing the ribs with the warmed basting sauce. Turn the ribs and continue brushing them with the basting sauce for another 10 minutes or until the meat pulls away from the bones with ease. (Note: Survey the ribs carefully while grilling to prevent burning, as sugar sauces burn easily.) Remove the ribs from heat and warm the remaining basting sauce over low heat. Transfer the sauce to a gravy dish or small bowl to serve with the ribs.

MAKES 2-3 SERVINGS.

Fresh Blackberry Pie

SWEET AND SYRUPY, THIS OLD-FASHIONED, LATTICE-TOPPED FAVORITE WILL TAME YOUR BIG, BAD MAN JUST A WEE BIT. OVERFLOWING WITH FORTIFYING BLACKBERRIES, IT'LL KEEP HIS ENGINE IDLING IN HIGH GEAR AND READY FOR ACTION DESPITE ITS SWEET APPEARANCE.

FOR THE CRUST:
1³/₄ cups all-purpose flour
¹/₄ cup cake flour
1 teaspoon salt
6 tablespoons (³/₄ stick) unsalted butter, well chilled and cut into pieces
¹/₄ cup lard, well chilled and cut into pieces
6 to 8 tablespoons ice water
1 egg white, well beaten

FOR THE FILLING:
3 8-ounce baskets blackberries
³/₄ cup sugar
1 teaspoon fresh lemon juice
¹/₄ cup all-purpose flour
2 tablespoons unsalted butter, cut into pieces
1 tablespoon sugar

Sift the flours for the crust into a large bowl. Add the salt and mix well. Cut in the butter and lard until the mixture resembles a coarse meal. Gradually add the water, one tablespoon at a time, until the dough gathers into a ball. Divide the dough in half and flatten each half into a disc. Wrap each disc and refrigerate for one hour.

Preheat the oven to 350 degrees F. Remove the dough from the refrigerator. On a lightly floured surface, roll one disc into an 11-inch round. Transfer to a 9-inch pie pan with 2-inch sides. Cover and refrigerate. Roll out the remaining disc into a 13-inch round and cut it into 1/2-inch-wide strips. Refrigerate. Remove the crust from the refrigerator and brush the bottom with egg white. In a small mixing bowl, combine the berries, sugar, and lemon juice. Gently toss with the flour and pour the mixture into the pie pan. Add the pieces of butter to the top of the berries and weave the dough strips across the top of the pie, pinching to seal the edges. Bake until the top crust is light brown, approximately 1 hour. Remove the pie from the oven and brush the lattice with the remaining egg white and sprinkle with sugar. Return to the oven and bake for an additional 10 minutes. Allow the pie to cool on a rack before serving.

MAKES 8 SERVINGS.

Chapter 3
The Eternal Peace Corps Officer

He carries the weight of the world on his shoulders, but will love with altruistic passion. Lighten his load and turn his activism toward you with this comforting soup and griddle cake combo. Your globetrotter understands an honest meal and abhors all things gimmicky and contrived, so keep it simple and delicious—grassroots flavors and earthy ingredients will be the key to enticing him. The hearty Turkey Barley Soup offers ample amounts of humble root vegetables, and dessert doesn't come more homegrown than a slab of pumpkin raisin cake with its no-frills icing of cream cheese and chopped nuts. In this menu, your respectful use of Mother Earth's historical wealth—turkey, barley, corn, pumpkin, and raisins—will soothe his social consciousness. It's a meal that screams "Peace" and "Love!"

THE SONG: *Give Peace a Chance* by John Lennon

THE BEVERAGE: Red Zinger Iced Tea with Unrefined Brown Sugar and an Orange Wedge

Turkey Barley Soup

THIS SOUP IS SO COMFORTING; IT WILL BRING YOUR THIRD WORLD LOVER HOME TO ROOST FOR GOOD. IT FEATURES THE NATIVE AMERICAN BIRD—TURKEY (PURCHASE AN ORGANIC, FREE-RANGE BIRD WHENEVER POSSIBLE)—AND IS CHOCK FULL OF THE HOME-STYLE VEGETABLES YOUR PEACE-LOVING MAN CERTAINLY MISSES WHEN HE'S GONE. NEARLY ALL SOUPS ARE BETTER SERVED THE DAY AFTER THEY ARE MADE, SO TRY TO ANTICIPATE WHEN YOU'LL BE BREAKING BREAD WITH YOUR MAN AND PREPARE THIS SOUP, UP TO THE ADDITION OF THE BARLEY, THE DAY BEFORE YOUR DATE.

1 meaty turkey carcass, quartered
9 celery stalks, chopped into ½-inch pieces
1 pound carrots, peeled and chopped into ½-inch rounds
2 onions, peeled and chopped into ½-inch pieces
½ pound parsnips, peeled and chopped into ½-inch pieces
6 cloves garlic, minced
¼ cup fresh sage
1 cup fresh parsley, chopped
1 tablespoon sea salt
2 teaspoons ground white pepper
1 cup barley
4 quarts water, plus more as needed

Place the turkey carcass, celery, carrots, onions, parsnips, garlic, sage, parsley, salt and pepper in a stockpot. Add water to cover and bring to a boil. Reduce heat and simmer for two hours, occasionally skimming the foam from the top of the stock. Remove the turkey carcass from the stock and set it aside to cool. Once cool enough to handle, remove the meat from the carcass and return the meat to the stockpot. Discard the carcass. Add the barley to the soup and simmer for 40 minutes or until the barley is tender. Add additional water as needed if soup is too thick. Taste and adjust seasonings if necessary. Serve hot. Leftovers may be frozen once fully cooled.

MAKES 8-10 SERVINGS.

Cornmeal Griddle Cakes

THESE SIMPLE, LIGHT CAKES WILL REMIND YOUR WORLD TRAVELER OF THE "REAL AMERICA" HE'S DETERMINED TO SERVE. THEY FEATURE THAT ELEMENTAL CORN FLAVOR, WITH A DECIDEDLY MORE LUXURIOUS "FIRST-WORLD" TEXTURE. HE'LL FLIP FOR THEM, AND YOU!

1 cup flour
1 cup cornmeal
1 teaspoon baking soda
1½ teaspoons salt
2 eggs
2 cups buttermilk
1 tablespoon light corn syrup

Mix the flour, cornmeal, baking soda, and salt together until well combined. In a separate bowl, beat the eggs until frothy and gradually add the buttermilk and corn syrup, stirring until well blended. Whisking continuously, gradually add the dry ingredients to the egg mixture and stir until thoroughly blended. Grease a griddle and heat. Spoon batter onto griddle, forming cakes measuring about 3 inches in diameter. Fry until golden brown on one side, flip and continue frying until the griddle cake is golden. Serve warm.

MAKES 2 SERVINGS.

Pumpkin Raisin Cake with Cream Cheese Icing

DENSE, EARTHY, AND RICH, THIS IS A SENSIBLE, STICK-TO-YOUR-RIBS SWEET THAT WILL SPEAK TO YOUR MAN'S SOFT SIDE AND SENSE OF RESTRAINT. SETTLE IN FOR A SNUGGLE AS SMOOTH AND SPICY AS THIS CAKE, PUNCTUATED BY LUSCIOUS CREAM CHEESE KISSES.

2 cups (one 16-ounce can) pumpkin
2 cups sugar
1 cup vegetable oil
4 eggs
2 cups self-rising flour
2 teaspoons baking soda
½ cup golden raisins
½ cup walnuts, chopped, plus more for garnishing
3 teaspoons cinnamon

Preheat the oven to 325 degrees F. In a mixing bowl, beat together the pumpkin, sugar, vegetable oil, and eggs. In a separate bowl, combine the flour, baking soda, raisins, walnuts, and cinnamon. Add the pumpkin mixture to the flour mixture and mix well. Pour into a well-greased and -floured tube pan and bake for 75 minutes. Do not overbake. Let cool completely and remove the cake from the pan. Frost the cake with cream cheese icing (recipe follows) and sprinkle with chopped walnuts.

MAKES 8-10 SERVINGS.

Cream Cheese Icing

16 ounces cream cheese, softened
1 stick of butter, softened
1 tablespoon pure vanilla extract
¼ cup whipping cream

Mix together the cream cheese, butter, vanilla, and whipping cream until smooth and creamy in texture. Use the icing immediately, or refrigerate. If the icing has been refrigerated, allow it to come to room temperature before frosting the cake. This will make the icing easier to spread.

Chapter 4
The Euro-Nerd

Debonair, hip, and just a little bit devilish,
this man's charms are thrillingly "out of this world." He's
one part bohemian, one part cutting edge, and makes
it no secret that he loves the chase. Put yourself in the
lead by treating him to a taste of café society. Begin
with a spare plate of Country French Pâté and wee cornichons—just the kind of appetite opener he'd find in
those picturesque inns he's so proud to frequent. Then
move to the wine-soaked Coq au Vin, a high-spirited
Burgundian specialty dressed up with an added flash of
brandy. Leeks Vinaigrette won't be foreign to this man,
and dessert shouldn't be too foolishly ooey and gooey.
Go continental on your suave sophisticate with the
exceedingly understated Parisian Apple Tart. Add a tiny
cup of robust espresso with a twist, and he'll feel right
at home here in the ol' USA.

THE SONG: *La Vie en Rose* by Edith Piaf

THE WINE: A well-balanced Côte du Rhone

Country French Pâté

YOUR EURO-NERD JUST MIGHT BETRAY HIS WELL-COMPOSED COOL WHEN YOU PULL THIS LOAF OF HOUSE-MADE PÂTÉ FROM THE FRIDGE. THIS MAKE-AHEAD APPETIZER GIVES YOU THE UPPER HAND IN THE GAME OF LOVE. DON'T ACT TOO TRIUMPHANT AS YOU SLICE IT UP AND SERVE. REMEMBER, YOUR EURO-NERD IS ALL ABOUT THE CHASE, AND WITH THIS MEAL OPENER, YOU'VE JUST SENT THE PROVERBIAL BALL SOARING INTO HIS COURT.

2 small onions
1 clove garlic
⅓ cup fresh parsley leaves
1½ pounds sliced bacon
¼ cup dry white wine
1 tablespoon cognac
1 teaspoon fines herbs
2 teaspoons salt
½ teaspoon coarsely ground black pepper
1 pound ground veal
1½ pounds ground pork
Cornichons (see Note)
Dijon mustard
Mixture of brown breads

Preheat the oven to 375 degrees F. Finely mince the onions, garlic, and parsley in a food processor. Add ½ pound of bacon, blending the mixture until smooth. Add the wine, Cognac, fines herbs, salt, and pepper and pulse until well mixed. Transfer this mixture to a large bowl and knead in the veal and pork. Line a 9 x 5-inch loaf pan with the remaining pound of bacon, allowing the bacon to hang over the edges of the pan. Firmly pack the pâté mixture into the pan, and fold the overhanging bacon across the top. Cover with a double layer of aluminum foil, and place the pan in a larger ovenproof pan of hot water. Bake for 1 hour and 45 minutes, or until the juices run clear. Remove the pâté from the pan of water and pour off the fat. Let the pâté cool, topped with a 2-pound weight. (An aluminum foil covered brick works perfectly.) Discard the outer layer of bacon if desired, and serve the pâté sliced thinly, with the cornichons, Dijon mustard, and bread medley. The pâté will keep, covered and refrigerated, for up to one week.

Note: Cornichons are tiny French gherkins, available in the condiment aisle of most specialty food grocery stores.

MAKES 10 SERVING WITH LEFTOVERS.

Coq au Vin

THERE'S NOTHING HOMELY ABOUT THIS ONE-DISH DINNER. CONSIDER FLAMING YOUR BIRD IN YOUR EURO MAN'S PRESENCE, THEN ENJOY AN APERITIF TOGETHER WHILE YOUR CHICKEN SIMMERS GENTLY. COME BACK INSIDE, ADD A BIT MORE VINO, AND *VOILÀ!*

2 slices bacon, diced
1 medium onion, chopped
2 carrots, chopped
2 tablespoons butter
1 chicken fryer, carved into pieces
Flour
Salt
Pepper
1½ tablespoons brandy
2 shallots, chopped
1 clove garlic, minced
¼ teaspoon thyme
¼ teaspoon marjoram
1 bay leaf
1 small cluster fresh parsley sprigs tied together
1½ cups Burgundy wine, plus more as needed

Lightly brown the bacon, onions, and carrots in the butter, then remove them from the pan. Coat the chicken with flour, salt, and pepper, and brown in the pan fat, adding more butter if necessary. Pour off any excess fat. (Note: This is an important step—absolutely necessary to avoid a grease fire!) Splash brandy over the chicken and ignite. When the flame dies out, return the bacon, carrots, and onion to the pot and add the shallots, garlic, thyme, marjoram, bay leaf, parsley, and the wine. Cover and cook gently over low heat until the chicken is tender, approximately 1 to 1½ hours, adding more wine as needed from time to time. Remove the bay leaf and parsley before serving. Serve with a crusty French baguette.

MAKES 6 SERVINGS.

Leeks Vinaigrette

AN OLD-FASHIONED CAFÉ FAVORITE THAT EXUDES HIP, RETRO APPEAL, LEEKS VINAIGRETTE IS A SALAD THAT WILL SPEAK TO YOUR EURO-NERD'S SENSE OF STYLE. TOSS A SMATTERING OF TINY, NONPAREIL CAPERS OVER THE TOP FOR AN ADDED TOUCH OF EURO CLASS, OR SERVE THE LEEKS ON A LARGE PLATTER, GARNISHED WITH PLUMP CAPERBERRIES ON STEMS.

15 leeks, with most of the green removed
Salt
Vinaigrette sauce (recipe follows)
Fresh parsley, chopped

Trim the leeks by removing most of the upper green portion of the stalk and cutting off a 1/4-inch section from the root end. Then make two 1-inch slices into the leek from the top down, and bottom up. Wash the leeks well by holding them under cold running water, carefully peeling back each layer of the stalk along the slices so that the water removes the sandy grit often found within the layers. Meanwhile, bring a large stockpot of salted water to a boil. Add the leeks, cooking until tender, approximately 15 minutes. (Do not overcook.) Remove the leeks from the pot and run them under cool water to stop the cooking. Allow the leeks to cool to room temperature, and slice them in half lengthwise. Dress with the vinaigrette and serve sprinkled with fresh chopped parsley.

MAKES 6 SERVINGS.

Vinaigrette

¼ cup fresh lemon juice
¾ cup extra-virgin olive oil
1 teaspoon salt
1 teaspoon freshly ground pepper

Combine the lemon juice, olive oil, salt, and pepper in a lidded jar, and shake until well blended.

Parisian Apple Tart

IT'S A CONTEMPORARY TAKE ON THE TARTE TATIN THAT YOUR MAN COULDN'T GET ENOUGH OF IN THOSE CHARMING LITTLE FRENCH BISTROS. THE KEY TO THIS DESSERT IS THE CARAMEL. MAKE SURE YOUR BUTTER AND SUGAR MIXTURE ATTAINS A DEEP AMBER COLOR BEFORE YOU POUR IT OVER THE TART.

FOR THE DOUGH:
2½ cups all-purpose flour
1 teaspoon sugar
1 teaspoon salt
2 sticks chilled unsalted butter cut into 1-tablespoon cubes
¼ cup ice water

In a food processor, combine the flour, sugar, and salt. Add the butter and pulse until the mixture resembles a coarse meal. With the food processor running, slowly pour the cold water through the feed tube and pulse until the dough sticks together, adding a bit more water only if needed for the dough to hold together without becoming sticky and wet, and without crumbling. Remove the dough from the processor and divide it into two equal pieces. Wrap with plastic wrap and chill for 1 hour. Use 1 dough ball for this recipe. The other may be frozen for another use.

TO PREPARE THE TART:
Chilled dough
8 small golden delicious apples, peeled, cored, and cut into ¼-inch wedges
½ cup fresh lemon juice
1 stick unsalted butter
½ cup sugar
½ cup heavy cream

Preheat the oven to 400 degrees F. Roll out the dough ball into a 9-inch round on a slightly floured work surface and transfer it to a baking sheet. Bake in the lower third of the oven for 10 minutes. Reduce the oven temperature to 375 degrees F and bake the crust for 10 minutes more, or until it is pale golden in color. Remove the crust from the oven and carefully transfer to a rack to cool. Do not turn off the oven. Meanwhile, toss the apples with the lemon juice in a small mixing bowl. Heat a large ovenproof skillet over high heat; add the butter and sugar and cook, stirring constantly, until the mixture turns a deep golden color. Carefully whisk in the cream (the mixture will splatter) and cook, whisking for an additional two minutes. Add the apples to the caramelized sugar and cream, and toss gently until well coated. Cover the caramelized apple mixture with foil and bake in the middle of the 375 degree F oven for 10 to 15 minutes, or until the apples are just tender. Remove from oven and arrange the apples, overlapping decoratively, on the tart shell. Bring the remaining caramel mixture to a boil, whisking continuously, for two minutes or until thickened and deep amber in color, and spoon over the apple tart. Serve à la mode with a dollop of vanilla bean ice cream in the center of the tart.

MAKES 6 SERVINGS.

Chapter 5
The Grill Master

He's hot under the collar, and you want to keep him that way. Fight fire with fire! Seduce your backyard pyromaniac with foods redolent of smoke. The porterhouse is the granddaddy of all steaks—certain to get your man's blood pumping with anticipation as it sizzles over the flames. Baked potatoes taste twice as good when they're twice baked, then spiked with chives and the sweet, mild taste of plump Vidalia onions. And a flame-kissed salad? It's a bowl of greens beyond your Grill Master's wildest dreams. Dessert will keep your flame's flame alive, firing him up with a generous shot of Jack Daniels folded into the sticky soft center of chocolate chip pecan pie. With results like this, your Grill Master will know you're the one—nearly too hot to handle!

THE SONG: *Breathless* by Faith Hill
THE WINE: Château Ste. Michelle Merlot

Grilled Radicchio and Endive

YOUR GRILL MASTER WON'T BELIEVE HIS GOOD FORTUNE WHEN PRESENTED WITH SALAD FARE BEARING THE TELLTALE MARKS OF THE GRILL. THE SEXY, SMOKY FLAVOR OF THESE GRILLED EURO "GREENS" WILL SEND HIM, SMOLDERING, STRAIGHT INTO YOUR ARMS.

1 head radicchio
1 head Belgian endive
1 tablespoon olive oil
1 tablespoon Balsamic vinegar
Sea salt
Freshly ground black pepper

Split the radicchio and endive heads lengthwise down the middle. Whisk together the olive oil and vinegar and brush evenly over the radicchio and endive. Sprinkle with salt and pepper, and grill, over medium heat, for four minutes on each side or until the heads are lightly marked with lines from the grill. Remove from heat and serve.

MAKES 2 SERVINGS.

Grilled Porterhouse Steaks

THIS IS A STEAK THAT WILL IMPRESS ANY AVID GRILL MAN OUT THERE, COMBINING THE MOST TENDER AND MOST FLAVORFUL CUTS OF BEEF IN A SINGLE STEAK. INSIST ON A PORTERHOUSE THAT IS 1½- TO 2-INCHES THICK, THE T-BONE BOASTING A FULL-SIZED FILET (THE MOST TENDER CUT) ON ONE SIDE AND A NICE STRIP STEAK WITH EVEN, CONSISTENT MARBLING (THE MOST FLAVORFUL CUT) ON THE OTHER. ASK YOUR BUTCHER FOR USDA PRIME GRADE STEAKS. IF PRIME IS UNAVAILABLE, ACCEPT NO GRADE LOWER THAN USDA CHOICE.

2 Porterhouse steaks, 1½- to 2-inches thick
Olive oil
Sea salt
Pepper
Worcestershire sauce

Remove the steaks from the refrigerator one hour prior to grilling and rub lightly on both sides with olive oil. Season with salt and pepper. Add several dashes of

Worcestershire sauce to each side of the steaks, and massage the sauce into the meat. Let the steaks sit, covered, at room temperature until you are ready to grill. Spray the grates of a gas or charcoal grill with cooking spray or wipe with oil. Heat the gas grill to high, or prepare a red-hot charcoal fire. Place the steaks on the gas grill over high heat, or approximately 6 inches above the glowing coals. The steaks should not come into contact with flames. If flames blaze up as a result of the meat drippings, extinguish them quickly with sprinkles of water. Grill the steaks for approximately 10 minutes, until they are nicely marked from the grate, then turn and continue grilling for another 7 to 10 minutes for medium-rare to medium. Grill an additional five minutes for medium well. Serve immediately.

MAKES 2 SERVINGS.

Perfect Potatoes

STEAK AND POTATOES HAS LONG BEEN A PERFECT MATCH, BUT PERFECTION CAN BE IMPROVED UPON. THESE POTATOES ARE THE PROOF. ELEVATE ORDINARY SPUDS TO SEXY, STEAMING NEW HEIGHTS WITH THE ADDITION OF SILKY COTTAGE CHEESE, FEISTY LITTLE CHIVES, AND THE GENTLE KICK OF THE SULTRY, SWEET VIDALIA ONION. THIS IS ONE OUT-OF-THE-OVEN TREAT YOUR GRILL MASTER WON'T BE ABLE TO RESIST.

1 large baking potato
6 tablespoons low-calorie cottage cheese
Several sprigs fresh chives, chopped fine
1 Vidalia onion, quartered and chopped
Salt
Pepper

Preheat the oven to 450 degrees F. Bake the potato for 45 minutes, then reduce the oven temperature to 275 degrees F and bake an additional 20 minutes. Remove the potato from the oven and set it aside until cool enough to handle. Once cool, cut it in half lengthwise and spoon out its flesh, leaving the potato skins intact. Mash the potato flesh in a small mixing bowl, leaving some chunks throughout, and delicately fold in the cottage cheese, chives, onions, salt, and pepper. Return the mixture to the potato skins, and broil the potatoes, watching them closely, for five minutes or until just golden.

MAKES 2 SERVINGS.

Jack Daniels Chocolate Chip Pecan Pie

SWEET AS SYRUP, SMOOTH AS SILK—THERE'S NO GETTING OVER THIS LUSCIOUS DESSERT. A SPIRITED DOSE OF JACK DANIELS UNLEASHES THIS PRIM SOUTHERN PIE'S WILD SIDE, AND WILL HAVE YOUR BACKYARD GRILL MASTER BEGGING TO GO BACK INSIDE.

3 extra-large eggs, slightly beaten
1 cup sugar
2 tablespoons unsalted butter, melted
1 cup dark corn syrup
2 teaspoons pure vanilla extract
¼ cup Jack Daniels whiskey
½ cup semi-sweet chocolate chips
1 cup whole pecans
1 10-inch store-bought pie crust, unbaked

Preheat the oven to 375 degrees F. In a mixing bowl, beat the eggs, sugar, butter, corn syrup, vanilla, and whiskey until well blended. Strain. Sprinkle chocolate chips over the bottom of the unbaked pie shell, cover with pecans, and pour in the egg mixture. Bake for 35 to 40 minutes, or until a knife inserted into the pie halfway between the pie's center and its crust comes out clean. Remove from oven and let pie cool at least 30 minutes before serving. Serve with a scoop of vanilla ice cream if desired.

MAKES 6 SERVINGS.

Chapter 6
Mr. Magnate

You see dollar signs when you stare into his eyes, and his fine, tailored clothes and cool, confident demeanor ooze good taste and class. Yes, your Daddy Warbucks is a good catch on two fronts, but enrapturing this reserved blue blood will be anything but easy. Offer him high style with no shimmer. Luxury without gaud. Carpaccio with Garlic Parsley Sauce to capture his attention. Swordfish au Poivre to keep it. And a Souffle au Grand Marnier as your final coup de grace. This menu presents classic flavors with just enough spice and originality to pique your Magnate's interest and whet his greater appetite. It will have you laughing all the way to the bank.

Carpaccio with Garlic-Parsley Sauce and Lemon Bread

YOUR SOPHISTICATE HAS SEEN IT ALL, SO DON'T TRY TO IMPRESS HIM WITH DRESSED-UP, OVER-THE-TOP FLAVORS. THIS SIMPLE APPETIZER IS THE ULTIMATE IN STRAIGHTFORWARD, NO-FUSS REFINEMENT. IF AVAILABLE, PURCHASE A USDA PRIME GRADE TENDERLOIN FROM YOUR BUTCHER. ITS QUALITY WILL SPEAK MILLIONS.

1½-pounds tenderloin, fat removed
3 tablespoons white vinegar
6 cornichons (See Note.)
1 cup fresh parsley, chopped
3 cloves garlic
2 anchovy fillets
3 tablespoons nonpareil capers, rinsed and drained
1 tablespoon shallot, chopped
1 tablespoon Dijon mustard
⅔ cup extra-virgin olive oil
Freshly ground black pepper

Briefly freeze the tenderloin until firm. When the meat is barely frozen, remove it from the freezer and slice it into paper-thin slices. Arrange the sliced meat on a serving platter and cover with transparent wrap, then chill it, until ready to serve. In the bowl of a food processor or blender, blend the vinegar, cornichons, parsley, garlic, anchovies, capers, shallot, and mustard until thoroughly combined. Gradually add olive oil to the mixture, one drop at a time while the machine is still running, and continue to blend until you obtain a smooth green sauce of medium thickness. Chill the sauce until ready to serve. To serve, drizzle several tablespoons of the sauce artfully over the carpaccio and top with freshly ground black pepper. Serve with Lemon Bread.

Note: Cornichons are tiny pickled gherkins from France. Look for them in the condiment aisle of your grocery store, or in the deli case at your specialty grocers.

MAKES 2 SERVINGS.

Lemon Bread

THIS IS THAT LITTLE SOMETHING EXTRA THAT WILL MAKE YOUR MAGNATE SMILE. IT'S THE ONE-OF-A-KIND TOUCH, THE *NE PLUS ULTRA* THAT HE JUST CAN'T LIVE WITHOUT. FAR MORE INTERESTING THAN CRACKERS, FAR MORE EXCITING THAN MERE BREAD, THIS CITRUS-Y LOAF IS THE SUBTLE GESTURE THAT WILL SEND YOUR CARPACCIO OVER THE TOP.

1/2 cup vegetable shortening
1 1/4 cups sugar
2 large eggs
1 1/4 cups all-purpose flour
1 teaspoon double-acting baking powder
1/4 teaspoon salt
1/2 cup milk
1/2 cup walnuts, chopped fine
1 teaspoon freshly grated lemon zest
1/4 cup fresh lemon juice

Preheat the oven to 350 degrees F. In a mixing bowl, cream the shortening and one cup of the sugar until the mixture is light and fluffy. Add the eggs one at a time, beating continuously until the mixture is smooth. In a separate bowl, sift the flour, baking powder, and salt. Gradually add the dry ingredients and the milk, alternately, into the egg mixture and stir until just combined. Add the walnuts and lemon zest and stir. Pour the batter into a well-buttered 9 x 5-inch loaf pan and bake in the middle of the oven for one hour, or until a toothpick inserted into the middle of the loaf comes out clean. Transfer the loaf pan to a wire rack to cool, and poke the loaf all over with a small skewer or toothpick. In a small mixing bowl, stir together the remaining 1/4 cup sugar and lemon juice. Pour the mixture over the hot bread and allow bread to cool completely in the pan before serving.

MAKES 6-8 SERVINGS.

Swordfish au Poivre with Cognac-Mustard Sauce

HE'S A BIG FISH IN A SMALL WORLD WHO WILL KNOW HE'S IMPRESSED YOU WHEN THIS FLAVOR-PACKED ENTRÉE IS PRESENTED. SWORDFISH GETS ROYAL TREATMENT HERE, AND WILL TANTALIZE EVEN THE MOST RESERVED OF GENTLEMEN WITH ITS FEISTY, PEPPERY EXTERIOR AND COGNAC-INFUSED SAUCE.

½ cup Cognac-Mustard sauce (recipe follows)
2 tablespoons black peppercorns, crushed
2 tablespoons pink peppercorns, crushed
2 8-ounce swordfish steaks, center cut with no brown meat
½ cup clarified butter (see Note)

Spread a small amount of Cognac-Mustard sauce over both sides of the swordfish steaks. Combine the black and pink peppercorns, and sprinkle half of the pepper over the swordfish steaks, pressing the pepper into the fish to coat it. Refrigerate for one hour. Preheat oven to 375 degrees F. Add the clarified butter to a skillet and heat to high. Sear the swordfish steaks for about 30 seconds on each side, or until the crushed peppercorns and mustard sauce form a crust. Transfer the fish to the oven and cook for 15 minutes more, or until just cooked through.

MAKES 2 SERVINGS.

Note: Clarified butter is made by melting butter and separating the transparent, golden butter from the heavier milk solids, which cause the butter to burn easily. To separate, skim the foam from the top of the warmed melted butter, then pour off the clear liquid into a separate container carefully so as not to disturb the heavier solids that will accumulate at the bottom of the pan.

Cognac-Mustard Sauce

1 cup Dijon mustard
2 tablespoons vegetable oil
2 tablespoons honey
2 teaspoons cognac

Blend the mustard, oil, honey, and cognac together in a blender or food processor. Use to coat fish before cooking and serve alongside cooked swordfish steaks.

MAKES 2 SERVINGS.

Soufflé Grand Marnier

END YOUR MEAL ON A DECIDEDLY HIGH NOTE WITH THIS GLAMOROUS, DECADENT DESSERT. GRAND MARNIER INFUSES THIS SWANKY VINTAGE DISH WITH THE SWEET SCENT OF ORANGES. CONSIDER POURING A SNIFTER OR TWO OF AROMATIC ARMAGNAC TO GO ALONG WITH THE SOUFFLÉ AND LET YOUR MAGNATE OFFER THE AFTER-DINNER TOAST.

7 egg whites
2 cups milk
3/4 cup sugar
1/3 cup flour
2 ounces butter, at room temperature
2 ounces Grand Marnier
5 egg yolks
1 small carton lightly whipped cream for topping

Preheat the oven to 400 degrees F, and generously butter a 6-cup soufflé dish. Beat egg whites until stiff. In a small saucepan, heat the milk until it just reaches a boil, lower the heat, and add the sugar. Watch carefully to avoid boiling over. In a separate mixing bowl mix together the flour and butter Add the butter mixture to the hot milk mixture and stir constantly until the mixture is creamy. Remove from heat and add the Grand Marnier. In a separate mixing bowl, beat the egg yolks. Add the yolks to the milk mixture and continue stirring. Gently fold in the egg whites. Pour into the buttered soufflé dish and bake for 20 to 25 minutes. Do not open the oven door until soufflé has risen and is ready to be removed. Remove from oven and top with light whipped cream. Serve immediately.

MAKES 2-4 SERVINGS.

Chapter 7
Mama's Boy

He's sweet as can be, but burdened by lofty filial expectations. You'll set him free right away with this soothing menu featuring old-fashioned flavors. There's a Fresh Berry Salad with a sensibly sweet Cinnamon Yogurt Dressing—a nostalgic nod to the family cradle and convivial Sunday dinners. Mushroom and Veal Meatloaf makes its entrance next, stylishly rescuing his old ketchup-topped childhood favorite. And the evening ends cozily, with a comforting, security-blanket kind of sweet—a bowl of Rice Pudding, its warm embrace as smooth and gentle as dear Mother's.

THE SONG: *Sweet Potato Pie* by Ray Charles and James Taylor

THE DRINK: Sweet Iced Tea and with dessert, Bailey's Irish Cream and coffee

Fresh Berry Salad with Sweet Cinnamon Yogurt Dressing

HE'LL BE SWEET ON YOU FROM THE GET-GO WHEN YOU LAUNCH YOUR LOVE AFFAIR OVER A WHOLESOME BOWL OF FRESH BERRIES MISCHIEVOUSLY SPIKED WITH GRAND MARNIER. THE SWEET CINNAMON YOGURT DRESSING GIVES THIS FRUITY TREAT GROWN-UP PANACHE. ONE SMOOTH SPOONFUL, AND HE'S BOUND TO WONDER JUST WHO HIS "MAMA" SHOULD BE!

2 pints fresh blueberries
1/2 pound fresh strawberries, stems removed and halved
1 pint fresh blackberries
1/4 cup Grand Marnier
1/4 cup sugar
1 pint fresh raspberries

In a mixing bowl, toss the blueberries, strawberries, and blackberries with the Grand Marnier and sugar. Transfer the fruit to a clear glass bowl and sprinkle the raspberries on top. Serve with Sweet Cinnamon Yogurt dressing (recipe follows).

Sweet Cinnamon Yogurt Dressing

1 cup plain yogurt
1 1/2 tablespoons confectioner's sugar
1/4 teaspoon cinnamon
1 tablespoon fresh mint, chopped

Combine the yogurt, sugar, and cinnamon in a small mixing bowl. Fold in the chopped mint, stir, and chill until ready to serve.

MAKES 4 SERVINGS.

Mushroom and Veal Meatloaf

HOMESPUN GOES HIGH STYLE WITH THE SIGNATURE DISH—A FRESH, HERB-LADEN LOAF OF VEAL AND MUSHROOMS—FROM ATLANTA'S FAVORITE EATERY, THE BUCKHEAD DINER. THIS IS MEAT-LOAF WITH CREATIVE FLAIR, SO GOOD IT'LL PUT HIS "THERE'S NO PLACE LIKE HOME" CONVICTION TO THE TEST! PLUS, IT MAKES FOR GREAT LEFTOVERS. SHARE THEM ON A FOLLOW-UP DATE FOR A HOMEY TOUCH HE WON'T FAIL TO NOTICE.

2 medium onions, chopped
1 shallot, chopped
$1\frac{1}{2}$ cloves garlic, minced
Olive oil
$\frac{1}{2}$ pound button mushrooms, sliced
$\frac{1}{4}$ pound shiitake mushrooms, quartered
$\frac{1}{8}$ pound oyster mushrooms, sliced thick
$2\frac{1}{2}$ pounds ground veal
1 cup heavy cream
2 eggs
One quarter of a bunch of flat leaf or Italian parsley, chopped fine
1 bunch fresh chives, chopped
$\frac{1}{4}$ bunch fresh thyme, chopped
$1\frac{1}{4}$ cups bread crumbs
1 tablespoon Worcestershire sauce
Salt
Pepper

Preheat the oven to 350 degrees F. Sauté the onions, shallots, and garlic in olive oil, and let cool. Sauté the mushrooms in olive oil and let cool. In a large mixing bowl, mix together the veal, cream, eggs, parsley, chives, thyme, bread crumbs, and Worcestershire sauce. Add the sautéed onions, shallots, and garlic and the sautéed mushrooms and mix until evenly incorporated. Salt and pepper to taste. Transfer to a 9 x 5-inch loaf pan and bake, covered, for 25 minutes. Reduce the oven temperature to 300 degrees F and continue baking, uncovered, for an additional 10 minutes or until browned.

MAKES 8 SERVINGS.

Old-Fashioned Rice Pudding

EVEN HIS DEAR, SWEET MAMA COULDN'T DO DESSERT THIS GOOD. SIMPLE, YET SIMPLY
DELICIOUS, THIS OLD-FASHIONED AFTER-DINNER (OR BREAKFAST!) FAVORITE IS AS SOFT
AND COMFORTING AS A WELL-WORN FAMILY QUILT. GET READY FOR SOME TENDER LOVING,
SPOONFUL AFTER SPOONFUL.

4 cups milk
1 cup converted rice
4 eggs
$\frac{1}{2}$ cup sugar
1 tablespoon butter, melted
$1\frac{1}{2}$ teaspoons vanilla
$\frac{1}{2}$ teaspoon salt
$\frac{1}{2}$ cup raisins
1 teaspoon nutmeg

Preheat the oven to 350 degrees F. Combine 2 cups of milk and the rice in a medium
saucepan and bring just to a boil. Turn the heat to low and cook 15 to 20 minutes, or
until the rice is tender. Remove from heat. In a small mixing bowl, beat the eggs well
and add the sugar. Continue beating. Add the remaining 2 cups milk, the butter,
vanilla, and salt, and blend well. Combine the cooled rice mixture with the egg mixture, and stir in the raisins. Pour the pudding into an 8 x 8-inch pan and dust the top
with nutmeg. Place the pudding pan in a larger pan filled with water. (Water should
reach about 2/3 of the way up the sides of the pudding pan.) Bake for 30 minutes or
until set.

MAKES 6-8 SERVINGS.

Chapter 8
The Music Man

He whistles while he walks, sings in the shower, and has a CD collection to rival a DJ's. Make yourself his favorite instrument. This harmonious menu is sure to strike the right chord. There's the upbeat Carrot and Orange Soup humming with curry and a hint of garlic, and sautéed Red Snapper gone soulful in its exotic pool of ginger, cilantro, soy, and sesame oil. Weigh in with Chilled Lemon Soufflé for a masterful grand finale. The citrusy top note of this trendy dessert is sure to get your evening off and swinging.

Carrot and Orange Soup

CURRY COMBINES WITH ORANGE JUICE AND ORANGE ZEST IN THIS BRIGHT MEAL OPENER CREATED EXPRESSLY FOR THE PURPOSE OF GETTING YOUR COURTSHIP OFF ON A HIGH NOTE. BESIDES BEING TASTY, THE INGREDIENTS IN THIS UNUSUAL SOUP MAKE FOR SUPREMELY SNAZZY EATING. THINK ORANGE! IT'S VIVID AND INVITING—AN ENERGIZING TONIC MEANT TO GET YOUR MUSIC MAN'S HEART BEATING IN DOUBLE TIME.

4 tablespoons butter or olive oil
4 to 6 medium carrots, peeled and chopped
2 onions, chopped
1 leek, white part only, chopped
1 teaspoon curry powder
1 garlic clove, chopped
Zest of 1 orange, no white pith
4 cups chicken stock
Juice of 2 oranges
Salt
Freshly ground white pepper
1 teaspoon brown sugar

Heat the butter or olive oil in a heavy-bottomed pan. Add the carrots, onions, and leek. Cover and cook over low heat for 10 minutes or until the onions are soft. Do not brown. Stir in curry powder and garlic and continue to cook. Add 1/2 of the orange zest, the chicken stock, and orange juice, and continue cooking until the carrots are tender. Remove the solids from the soup pot using a slotted spoon and puree them in a food processor until smooth. Return the puree to the pot and stir well to combine. Add the salt, pepper, sugar, and the remaining orange zest to the soup and stir.

MAKES 6 SERVINGS.

Red Snapper in Ginger-Cilantro Vinaigrette

FOR FISH WITH AN ASIAN GROOVE, THIS RED SNAPPER'S GINGER-CILANTRO VINAIGRETTE IS OUTTA SIGHT. YOU'LL WANT TO MAKE A DOUBLE BATCH TO KEEP ON HAND FOR JAZZING UP SAUTÉED CHICKEN BREASTS OR WEEKDAY SANDWICHES. FOR YOUR MUSIC-LOVING MAN, POOL THE VINAIGRETTE ON THE PLATE, SERVE YOUR SNAPPER ON TOP, AND SIT BACK AND LISTEN TO HIS RAVE REVIEWS. FISH LIKE THIS IS SURE TO TOP HIS CHART.

1 1-inch knob fresh ginger root, peeled and minced
2 large shallots, minced
¼ cup rice wine vinegar
1 cup extra-virgin olive oil
Juice of 2 limes
2 tablespoons soy sauce
2 tablespoons dark sesame oil
Salt
Freshly ground white pepper
4 red snapper fillets, approximately 6 ounces each
1 bunch cilantro, roughly chopped, plus a few whole sprigs for garnishing
¼ cup black sesame seeds

In a small mixing bowl or lidded jar, combine the ginger, shallots, vinegar, olive oil, lime juice, and soy sauce. Add the sesame oil and whisk vigorously until combined. Add salt and pepper to taste, and set aside, keeping the vinaigrette at room temperature. Season the fish fillets on both sides with salt and pepper, and sauté over high heat in a splash of olive oil or tablespoon of butter for 1 to 2 minutes. Remove from heat, add the chopped cilantro to the vinaigrette, and dress the fish, garnishing the plate with a smattering of black sesame seeds and a sprig of fresh cilantro.

MAKES 4 SERVINGS.

Chilled Lemon Soufflé

CONTINUING THE CITRUS RIFF BEGUN WITH THE SOUP, THIS CHILLED LEMON SOUFFLÉ WILL BRING YOUR MUSIC MAN'S MENU TO A CLOSE IN A DAZZLING CRESCENDO. THIS SNAPPY DESSERT SHOULD BE MADE AHEAD OF TIME AND DECORATED AS A DUET. PRESENT AN ENSEMBLE OF TOPPINGS TO CHOOSE FROM, INCLUDING CHOPPED PISTACHIOS AND SLIVERED ALMONDS, MACAROON CRUMBS, AND OF COURSE, A GENEROUS HELPING OF SMOOTH, SILKY WHIPPED CREAM.

6 large eggs, separated, plus 1 additional egg white
1½ cups sugar

²/₃ cup lemon juice
Zest of 1 lemon
2 cups heavy cream, lightly whipped
2 tablespoons gelatin dissolved in ¹/₂ cup cold water
Pistachios
Almond slivers
Macaroons
Whipped cream

In a medium saucepan over low heat, whisk the egg yolks, 1 cup of the sugar, the lemon juice, and lemon zest until the mixture forms into a smooth mousse-like consistency. Taste for seasoning, and add the additional 1/2 cup sugar if necessary, whisking continuously. Remove from heat and continue to beat until cool. Add the lightly whipped heavy cream and blend well. Warm the gelatin over low heat, allow to cool a bit, and add it to the lemon-cream mixture. Stir the mixture in a mixing bowl set inside a larger bowl filled with ice. Once the mixture has thickened, beat the egg whites until stiff but not dry, and gently fold them into the lemon-cream. When well incorporated, gently transfer the mousse to a collared soufflé dish, and refrigerate until firm, approximately 4 hours. To serve, remove the collar and garnish.

MAKES 8 SERVINGS.

Chapter 9
The Rugged Outdoorsman

Rough, weathered, and positively delicious *au naturel*, this guy has got it in for all things earthy and elemental. With this menu, you'll give him a walk on the wild side he won't soon forget. Get things sizzling with a Hot Bacon Spinach Salad, then appeal to the hunter-gatherer in him with a savory Roasted Wild Duck paired with Wild Rice. Sweet, bubbling Georgia Peach Pie should soften his rough edges, but keep him far from tame—rugged and ready, just like you like him.

THE SONG: *Born to Be Wild* by Steppenwolf

THE WINE: Robert Mondavi Napa Valley Pinot Noir Reserve

Hot Bacon Spinach Salad

TENDER FRESH SPINACH LEAVES TAKE ON A RUSTIC EDGE WHEN TOPPED WITH BACON, HARD-BOILED EGGS, AND A SINFULLY GOOD BACON FAT–INFUSED DRESSING. THIS SALAD'S WARMED VINAIGRETTE WILTS THE SPINACH LEAVES ON CONTACT, SO CORRAL YOUR OUTDOORSMAN AT THE TABLE BEFORE DRESSING IT, AND SERVE THIS SALAD IMMEDIATELY.

8 slices bacon
2 bunches (or 2 bags) fresh spinach, washed, dried, and torn into bite-sized pieces
3 scallions, chopped fine
3 hard-boiled eggs, chopped
4 tablespoons vinegar or fresh lemon juice
1 teaspoon sugar
½ teaspoon Dijon mustard
Salt
Freshly ground black pepper

Fry the bacon in a skillet and reserve the fat in a small saucepan. Drain the bacon on a paper towel–lined plate and crumble it once dried. In a chilled salad bowl, combine the spinach leaves, scallions, eggs, and bacon and refrigerate. Add the vinegar or lemon juice, sugar, and mustard to the reserved bacon fat, season with salt and pepper, and warm over low heat, stirring to dissolve the sugar. When the sugar has dissolved remove the dressing from heat, allow it to cool for a minute or two, and pour over the spinach salad. Serve immediately.

MAKES 6 SERVINGS.

Roasted Wild Duck

HE'LL COME IN FROM THE WILDS FOR THIS AUTUMNAL TREAT. GET A FIRE CRACKLING IN THE FIRE-PLACE AND A BEEFY WOOLEN BLANKET OUT FOR SNUGGLING WHILE YOUR DUCK IS ROASTING TO GOLDEN PERFECTION. BASTE YOUR BIRD OFTEN TO ENSURE MOIST, FLAVORFUL MEAT. ANY RUGGED OUTDOORSMAN, HUNTER OR NOT, WILL APPRECIATE ROASTED DUCK FOR ITS EARTHY (AS OPPOSED TO GAMEY) FLAVOR, AND ITS SATISFYING, STICK-TO-YOUR-RIBS TEXTURE.

1 5-pound Long Island duck
Salt
Freshly ground black pepper
1 apple, quartered
2 oranges, one quartered, one sliced
1 large carrot, roughly chopped
2 stalks celery with leaves
1 medium onion, halved
1 cup red wine
Water as needed

Preheat the oven to 350 degrees F. Wash and dry the duck thoroughly and salt and pepper its skin generously. Salt the inside of the duck's cavity, and then stuff it with the apple and orange quarters, carrot pieces, celery stalks, and half of the onion. Place the duck, breast side up, in a heavy-bottomed roasting pan with a fitted top. (Note: Enameled pans cook faster than metal ones.) Add the wine to the pan and then the water as needed for the liquid to reach the level of the duck's wing tips. Cover the duck breast with the sliced oranges and bake, basting regularly with pan juices, for 4 to 4½ hours or until the breast is tender and juices run clear. Remove the duck from the oven, uncover the pan, and return the duck to the oven for approxi-mately 30 minutes or until the skin has become golden brown and crisp. Allow the meat to sit approximately 5 minutes before carving.

MAKES 6-8 SERVINGS.

Wild Rice

YOUR RUGGED OUTDOORSMAN MAY NEVER HAVE FORAGED WILD RICE HIMSELF, BUT HE'LL NOTE YOUR NOD TO NATIVE TRADITION WITH THIS MOUND OF DENSE, HEARTY GRAINS. A THANKS- GIVING FAVORITE THE PILGRIMS PURPORTEDLY LEARNED TO LOVE FROM THEIR NATIVE AMERICAN COUNTERPARTS, WILD RICE WILL BRING OUT THE SAVAGE IN YOUR MAN. NOW THERE'S SOME- THING FOR WHICH TO BE THANKFUL!

2 cups water
1 cup wild rice
4 tablespoons unsalted butter, melted
Fresh thyme
Salt
Freshly ground black pepper

Combine the water and rice in medium saucepan over high heat. Bring the rice to a boil, then reduce the heat and simmer for 35 to 40 minutes or until the rice is tender to taste. Drain off any remaining water, and return the rice to the saucepan. Add the melted butter, fresh thyme, salt, and pepper, and stir to combine. Serve immediately.

MAKES 4 SERVINGS.

Georgia Peach Pie

AS RIPE AND JUICY AS A FUZZY ORB JUST PLUCKED FROM THE TREE, THIS PEACH PIE WILL HAVE YOUR RUGGED OUTDOORSMAN SALIVATING. KEEP THE MOOD SWEET BY SPOON-FEEDING YOUR MR. RIGHT HIS SECOND HELPING. EVEN *HE'LL* STAY PUT INSIDE WITH THE PROMISE OF TENDER, PEACH-LADEN KISSES.

³/₄ cup all-purpose flour
1 cup sugar
¹/₂ cup packed brown sugar
¹/₂ teaspoon ground cinnamon
Juice of 1 lemon
10 cups freshly sliced, firm peaches
1 all-purpose frozen deep-dish pie shell
Cinnamon topping (recipe follows)

Preheat the oven to 375 degrees F. Mix together the flour, sugar, brown sugar, and cinnamon. In a separate, large mixing bowl, combine the sliced peaches and lemon juice. Add the dry ingredients to the peaches and mix well. Transfer the peach mix- ture to an unbaked, deep-dish, 10-inch pie shell and cover with cinnamon topping (recipe follows.) Bake for 30 minutes or until topping is light brown. Serve warm.

CINNAMON TOPPING
2 cups all-purpose flour
2 cups sugar
2 teaspoons ground cinnamon
1 cup cold unsalted butter

Combine the flour, sugar, and cinnamon and mix well. Cut in the cold butter and blend until mixture forms small crumbles. Keep cool until ready to top pie.

MAKES 8 SERVINGS.

Chapter 10
The Starving Artist

He's all about "vision"; relentlessly focused in his drive to create. Color his palate with exotic flavors. Inspire his passion. Be his muse. Begin with Asian minimalism, presenting small plates layered with complementary flavors and varying textures. Add dimension by painting these little dishes—Curried Peanut Chicken and Hunan Pork Dumplings—with delectable sauces, masterpieces in their own right. Then shock him with beautiful simplicity. Zesty Zucchini is a study in green, flecked with fresh scallions and bright, leafy basil. You'll continue to buoy his spirits with an old-school French dessert. A classic perhaps, the Floating Island is far from stodgy. It's neo-contemporary and inspiring, kinetic and sculptural, not to mention downright divine!

Curried Peanut Chicken

A NO-FAIL RECIPE FOR SUCCESS, THESE CURRIED PEANUT CHICKEN BITES WILL STAVE OFF YOUR ARTIST'S HUNGER, BUT AMP UP HIS APPETITE—THE KIND OF SUBTLE, MULTI-FACETED APPROACH TO FOOD HE LOVES. ADD THE PEANUT, RAISIN, AND CILANTRO LEAVES IN AN ARTFUL FLOURISH. PRESENTATION IS MORE THAN HALF THE EQUATION WHEN IT COMES TO WOOING THIS MAN.

2 whole boneless, skinless chicken breasts (4 split breast halves)
1½ cups milk
¾ cup mayonnaise (preferably Hellmann's)
1½ tablespoons mango chutney
1 tablespoon dry sherry
½ tablespoon sherry vinegar
1 tablespoon plus ½ teaspoon curry powder
½ teaspoon turmeric
½ cup roasted salted peanuts, chopped fine
½ cup raisins
½ cup fresh cilantro, leaves only

Preheat the oven to 350 degrees F. Place the chicken breasts in a single layer in a shallow baking dish (or dishes) and pour milk over the chicken to cover it. Bake for 30 minutes, then remove the chicken from the milk and allow it to cool. Cut the chicken into 1-inch cubes and set aside in a mixing bowl. In a food processor fitted with a metal blade, blend together the mayonnaise, chutney, sherry, vinegar, curry powder, and turmeric. Pour the mayonnaise mixture over the chicken and toss to coat. Skewer the cubes with colored toothpicks or pre-soaked bamboo skewers and arrange on a serving platter. Sprinkle the peanuts, raisins, and cilantro over the chicken, and serve.

MAKES APPROXIMATELY 30 PIECES.

Hunan Pork Dumplings with Hot Sauce

THESE EXQUISITE LITTLE POUCHES OF PORK ARE A LABOR OF LOVE, BUT YOUR EFFORTS WON'T GO UNAPPRECIATED BY YOUR WORLDLY AESTHETE. THE DUMPLING FILLING MAY BE MADE AHEAD OF TIME AND REFRIGERATED TO SPEED THE PROCESS, BUT CUT NO CORNERS WHEN IT COMES TO SERVING. THINK LIKE A FOOD STYLIST: THE DUMPLINGS ARE STARKLY BEAUTIFUL SWIMMING IN AN

INK BLOT–INSPIRED POOL OF DIPPING SAUCE OR GLISTENING UP FROM THE DEPTHS OF A
CERAMIC BOWL, SPECKLED WITH SESAME SEEDS AND SCALLIONS.

FOR THE FILLING:
½ pound Napa cabbage, chopped fine
¾ pound ground pork
1 tablespoon fresh ginger, minced fine
¼ cup scallions, chopped (both green and white parts)
1 tablespoon soy sauce
1 tablespoon Chinese rice wine
1 tablespoon light sesame oil
1 teaspoon kosher salt
¼ teaspoon freshly ground black pepper

FOR THE DIPPING SAUCE:
¼ cup soy sauce
2 tablespoons rice vinegar
2 teaspoons light sesame oil
2 teaspoons red chili flakes or 1 teaspoon Chinese red chili sauce
Pinch of sugar

1 package wonton skins
1 egg white mixed with 2 teaspoons water
2 tablespoons scallions, cut into thin rounds, both green and white parts
2 tablespoons black sesame seeds

Combine the filling ingredients in a large mixing bowl and stir until well blended.
Place six to eight wonton skins on a clean work surface, and top each with 1 tablespoon of the filling. Beat 1 egg white with 2 teaspoons water, and brush the edges of
each wonton skin with the egg white mixture. Fold the wonton skin over to form a
triangular pillow, and seal well by pressing the edges together firmly with your fingertips, removing any air bubbles. Set aside on waxed paper and repeat process until
you have filled 24 wonton skins. Boil water gently in a large saucepan and add the
dumplings. When the water returns to a boil, watch carefully until the wontons float
to the top—at this point they are ready as they start to become slightly transparent.
Meanwhile, combine the ingredients for the dipping sauce, and transfer to warm
serving bowls or plates. Remove the dumplings from the heat, drain well, and serve,
garnished with freshly chopped scallions and black sesame seeds.

MAKES 4–6 SERVINGS.

Zesty Zucchini

A COLOR PALETTE ON THE PLATE, THIS STARKLY SOPHISTICATED VEGETARIAN OFFERING WILL HAR-NESS YOUR ARTIST'S AMOROUS CREATIVITY. GREEN IS THE COLOR OF BALANCE AND WELL BEING, A HUE FAVORED FOR ITS POSITIVE ENERGY. THE COLOR GREEN FUELS THE DESIRE TO EXPAND OR INCREASE. NEED WE SAY MORE? GREEN LIGHT IS A *GO!*

4 tablespoons butter
2 pounds firm zucchini, sliced into $\frac{1}{8}$-inch rounds
1 bunch green onions, chopped
2 tablespoons butter
2 tablespoons extra virgin olive oil
Salt
Pepper
$\frac{1}{4}$ teaspoon sugar
$\frac{1}{4}$ teaspoon dried basil

Melt the butter and olive oil and add the zucchini, basil, and green onions, sautéing over medium-high heat for approximately 6 minutes or until the zucchini has soft-ened, but is still vivid green in color. Add salt and pepper to taste and stir. Add the sugar and toss to combine. Remove from heat and serve.

MAKES 6 SERVINGS.

Floating Island

FUNKY AND FESTIVE, THIS EGG WHITE CONCOCTION IS THE IDEAL DESSERT FOR YOUR STARVING ARTIST. IT DISPLAYS FRUGALITY AND CREATIVITY—WHO KNEW YOU COULD MAKE SUCH A SENSA-TIONAL DESSERT WITH EGG WHITES? THE RASPBERRY SAUCE ADDS THAT PUNCH OF COLOR YOUR AESTHETE WILL APPRECIATE, AND THE CARAMEL OFFERS ADDED TASTE DIMENSION.

6 egg whites
1 cup sugar
2 cups fresh raspberries
1 12-ounce jar raspberry preserves
$\frac{1}{4}$ cup sugar
$\frac{1}{4}$ cup corn syrup

Beat the egg whites until firm and gently fold in the sugar. Heat a pan of water to 170 degrees F. Using an ice cream scoop, shape the egg whites into egg-shaped mounds and drop gently into the water to poach for 1 to 1$\frac{1}{2}$ minutes per side. (Tip: The egg whites won't turn over unless done on one side.) Remove from the water and allow to cool. Place the raspberries in the bowl of a food processor fitted with the metal blade. Add the preserves and pulse 10 to 15 seconds, or until smooth. Place the raspberry sauce in the bottom of a serving dish and arrange the cooled egg whites on top. In a small saucepan, combine the sugar and corn syrup and cook over medium-high heat until a caramel forms. Dip the tines of a dinner fork into the caramel and then drizzle the caramel strings over the egg white mounds. Do not refrigerate, but keep cool until ready to serve.

MAKES 6 SERVINGS.

Chapter 11
Mr. All-Nighter

Trapped in the 1980s club scene, carbohydrates fuel this party animal and soak up his alcohol intake. A challenge for even the most affirmed of night owls, Mr. All-Nighter keeps his jets perpetually fueled and ready for takeoff. He's not one to linger over dinner. In fact, getting this fun, noncommittal man to a private home is no easy feat. He prefers public spaces, neon lights, and undulating crowds, so be sure to invite another couple with staying power to join you for a late night of noshing and name-dropping. Handy, bite-sized food is a necessity. This American-Italian menu, with its homemade pizza-by-the-slice, a titillating pile of pop-'em-in-your-mouth fried calamari rings, and chocolate tiramisu for dessert, will kick his motor into overdrive. Make him think he's at Spago, rubbing shoulders with Don Johnson.

THE SONG: *Just a Gigolo* by Louis Prima

THE BEVERAGE: Ruffino Chianti Classico Reserve followed by Red Bull and Vodka

Pizza with Five Cheeses

YOUR MR. ALL-NIGHTER IS A LONER BY CHOICE, YET FINDS NO CONTRADICTION IN SURROUND-ING HIMSELF WITH A HAPPENING CROWD. THIS FIVE-CHEESE PIZZA PIE IS IDEAL FOR THE MAN WHO JUST CAN'T SIT DOWN. HE'LL BE TOTING HIS SLICE ALL OVER YOUR HOUSE, PEERING AT YOUR PHOTOS, ANALYZING YOUR ART, AND GENERALLY REVVING UP FOR AN EVENING FILLED WITH FUN AND FRENZY.

FOR THE DOUGH:
3 cups all-purpose flour
1 teaspoon salt
1 tablespoon honey
2 tablespoons olive oil
3/4 cup cool water
1 package active dry yeast
1/4 cup warm water
Butter for greasing bowl

Place the flour in a food processor. In a measuring cup, combine the salt, honey, olive oil, and cool water and mix well. Dissolve the yeast in the warm water and set aside to proof for 10 minutes. With the motor of the food processor running, slowly pour the honey mixture through the feed tube. Add the dissolved yeast and continue processing until the dough forms into a ball on the blade. If the dough seems sticky, gradually add flour until it holds its shape. Transfer the dough to a lightly floured work surface and knead it until smooth. Place the dough in a buttered bowl and set it aside for 30 minutes. Divide the dough into four equal parts, roll each piece into a smooth, tight ball, and place the balls on a baking sheet, making sure to space them far apart from one another. Cover the dough with a damp dishcloth and refrigerate. One hour before baking, remove the dough from the refrigerator and allow it to come to room temperature. Lightly flour a work surface. Using the fleshy part of your fingertips, flatten each ball into a circle approximately six inches in diameter, making the outer edge of the circle slightly thicker than the center. Turn the dough over and repeat this process. Lift the dough from the work surface and gently stretch its edges, working clockwise, in order to form an 8-inch circle. Place the dough rounds on a lightly floured wooden pizza peel or baking sheet and top it.

FOR THE TOPPING:
¼ cup Gorgonzola cheese, crumbled
½ cup mozzarella, shredded
½ cup plain goat cheese, sliced
½ cup sharp white cheddar, shredded
¼ cup Parmesan Reggiano, grated
5 fresh sage leaves, torn into small pieces
Salt
Freshly ground black pepper
2 tablespoons olive oil

Place a clean pizza stone in your oven and preheat it for 30 minutes to 475 degrees F. Cover 1/4 of the dough round with the Gorgonzola, 1/4 of the round with mozzarella, 1/4 with the goat cheese, and the remaining 1/4 with the white cheddar, careful to leave the outer edge of the round free of cheese. Sprinkle the entire pizza with the sage, and salt and pepper to taste. Drizzle olive oil evenly over the top. Repeat with the other 3 pizzas. Bake on the preheated pizza stone for 15 to 20 minutes or until the crust is light brown and the cheese bubbling. Remove the pizza from the oven and sprinkle its entirety with grated Parmesan cheese. Cut into slices and serve immediately.

MAKES 4 SERVINGS.

Salt and Pepper Fried Calamari

MR. ALL-NIGHTER LOVES A BAR'S ROARING CROWD, BUT CAN PASS ON THE STANDARD BEER AND MIXED NUTS FARE. FAR FROM HO-HUM, THESE SIMPLY SEASONED CALAMARI RINGS WILL MAKE HIM FEEL LIKE HE'S RAGING THROUGH A ROMAN HOLIDAY, GRABBING QUICK SUSTENANCE BEFORE ZIPPING OFF FOR THE DANCE FLOOR. DON'T HOLD BACK ON THESE LITTLE MOUTHFULS OF FUN. MAKE A DOUBLE BATCH IN HOPES OF HOLDING HIS ATTENTION AS LONG AS YOU CAN.

1 pound calamari tubes, cut into 1/2-inch rings
1 1/2 cups flour
2 tablespoons chili powder
2 tablespoons sugar
1 teaspoon cayenne pepper
1 teaspoon salt
1/2 teaspoon garlic powder
1/2 teaspoon onion powder
Peanut oil (no substitutions)
Store-bought marinara sauce for dipping

Mix together the flour, chili powder, sugar, cayenne pepper, salt, garlic powder, and onion powder in a large mixing bowl. Add the calamari rings and toss vigorously to coat. In a deep fryer, heat the peanut oil to 350 degrees F and add the calamari. Fry for approximately 3 minutes or until lightly browned. (Do not overcook or the calamari will become tough and rubbery.) Remove the calamari from the oil using a slotted spoon, drain, and serve with your favorite store-bought marinara sauce for dipping.

MAKES 4 SERVINGS.

Chocolate Tiramisu

THIS TRENDY ITALIAN DESSERT WARRANTS ITS NAME. "TIRAMISU" LITERALLY MEANS "PICK ME UP"—A FITTING NAME FOR A DESSERT CUSTOM-MADE FOR MEN LIKE YOUR MR. ALL-NIGHTER. IN THE PERFECT SELF-FULFILLING PROPHECY, THIS ESPRESSO-INFUSED CAKE WILL LIFT UP YOUR MAN, AND HAVE HIM "PICKING UP" ON YOU! PREPARE THIS DESSERT THE DAY BEFORE SERVING.

3 eggs
1 tablespoon Tia Maria or brandy
1 mascarpone cheese, at room temperature
1/2 cup sugar
2 packages ladyfinger biscuits, left out overnight to turn stale
1/2 cup brewed espresso or strong coffee
3 ounces semisweet chocolate, grated

Separate the three eggs into two bowls. Beat the liqueur into the egg yolks until they are pale yellow, then blend in the mascarpone. Beat the egg whites until they form soft peaks, and gradually add the sugar while continuing to beat. Blend 1/2 of the egg white mixture into the cheese mixture. Fold in the remaining egg whites and set aside. Brush the stale ladyfingers with the coffee, but do not saturate the ladyfingers. Layer the bottom of a 9 x 13-inch cake pan or serving platter with the ladyfingers. Add half of the cheese mixture and smooth until flat. Cover with 1/2 of the grated chocolate and repeat the layering process, ending with the chocolate. Cover and refrigerate overnight.

MAKES 10 SERVINGS.

Chapter 12
Mr. Culture Vulture

This man can hold court on just about any subject, and never ceases to amaze you with his knowledge, but a braggart he is not. Mr. Culture Vulture is discreet and unflinching—a man of letters and music, fine wines and far-reaching travels, political analyses and the studio arts . . . *en bref*, a walking liberal arts education. There's not much Mr. Culture Vulture hasn't kept up with, the culinary arts included, so regale him with timeless classics like an herb-crusted rack of lamb with its vibrant fresh mint sauce and uncomplicated sides that showcase your kitchen know-how. This is a man who finds fusion food foolish (though he'd never say so out loud). Your best bet? Treat Mr. Culture Vulture to the best quality ingredients, and allow them to shine on their own, with only the slightest additions of herbs and aromatics.

Rack of Baby Lamb with Herbed Dijon Crust

SIMPLE ELEGANCE WITH AFFIRMED FLAVORS, RACK OF LAMB SPEAKS TO MR. CULTURE VULTURE'S INNATE SENSE OF STYLE. HE'S TRAVELED THE WORLD OVER AND PRETTY MUCH SEEN IT ALL WHEN IT COMES TO DINNER ENTREES, BUT YOU'LL WOO HIM NONETHELESS WITH THIS REGAL RACK OF GOLDEN-CRUSTED LAMB. SERVED MEDIUM-RARE AND DELICATELY DRIZZLED WITH MINT SAUCE, THIS IS A DINNER CENTERPIECE THAT EMBODIES HIS CULINARY PREFERENCE FOR FINE FOOD WITHOUT THE FUSS.

1 rack of baby lamb
1 cup white bread crumbs
½ cup fresh flat-leaf parsley, chopped fine
1 garlic clove, minced
3 tablespoons Dijon mustard
1 teaspoon Kosher salt
1 teaspoon freshly ground black pepper
2½ tablespoons extra-virgin olive oil

Preheat the oven to 400 degrees F. Carefully trim the rack of lamb, leaving the rib bones as long as possible. Leave approximately 1/4 inch of fat on the outside of the rack. Cut neat crisscrosses in the fat using a sharp knife. In a small mixing bowl, combine the bread crumbs, parsley, garlic, mustard, salt, and pepper, and add olive oil gradually until the mixture begins to hold together, yet still crumbles. Place the rack of lamb in a roasting pan and roast for 15 minutes. Remove the lamb and reduce the heat to 375 degrees F. Pat the bread crumb mixture evenly on both the meaty and fatty sides of the rack of lamb to form a crust approximately 1/4-inch thick. Return the lamb to the oven and roast for an additional 25 minutes or until just medium rare.

MAKES 2 SERVINGS.

Mint Sauce

JUST FEISTY ENOUGH FOR YOUR CULTURE VULTURE, THIS FRESH MINT SAUCE OFFERS A WORLD OF IMPROVEMENT OVER THE COLOR ADDED MINT JELLIES YOU FIND IN YOUR GROCERY AISLE. FOR OPTIMUM FRESHNESS AND FLAVOR, DON'T ADD THE MINT UNTIL YOU ARE READY TO SERVE THE LAMB.

¼ cup brown sugar
4 tablespoons water
½ cup cider vinegar
½ cup apple jelly
½ cup fresh mint, chopped fine

Combine the brown sugar, water, and vinegar in a small saucepan and cook over medium heat until the liquid is reduced by a third. Add the apple jelly and stir to combine well. Keep warm until ready to serve. Just prior to serving, stir in the chopped mint and remove from heat.

MAKES 3/4 CUP.

Braised Garlic String Beans

OTHERWISE HOMEY GREEN BEANS GO UPTOWN WHEN PAIRED WITH GENTLY BRAISED WHOLE CLOVES OF GARLIC. USE FRENCH HARICOTS VERTS IF AVAILABLE. OTHERWISE, PURCHASE YOUNG STRING BEANS AND HALVE THEM LENGTHWISE, FRENCH-STYLE. MR. CULTURE VULTURE WILL APPRECIATE YOUR NOD TO GALLIC TRADITION.

1 pound tender young string beans, trimmed, or 1 pound haricots verts
3 tablespoons unsalted butter
4 to 5 large whole garlic cloves
1 teaspoon fresh sage, chopped fine
1 tablespoon fresh flat-leaf parsley, chopped
Salt
Freshly ground black pepper

Cook the beans in boiling water until just tender, approximately 3 to 4 minutes. Drain, then rinse the beans under cold running water until fully cooled. Set the beans aside in a colander to drain fully. Meanwhile, melt the butter in a large skillet over low heat and add the whole garlic cloves. Cook, uncovered, until the garlic is lightly browned and soft, approximately 20 to 25 minutes. Do not allow butter to burn. Mash the softened garlic with a fork and blend into butter. Add the beans to the skillet and toss over medium heat, until thoroughly warmed. Add the sage, parsley, salt, and pepper. Toss to coat, and serve immediately.

MAKES 4 SERVINGS.

Tomates Provençales

ANOTHER NOD TO FRANCE AND ITS CULTURE OF GASTRONOMY, THESE STUFFED TOMATOES ARE A GREAT MAKE-AHEAD DISH TO COMPLEMENT LAMB, BEEF, OR ROASTED PORK LOIN. USE THE FRESHEST TOMATOES POSSIBLE (IN WINTER MONTHS, PURCHASE HYDROPONICALLY GROWN VARIETIES). MR. CULTURE VULTURE WILL LAUD THIS DISH'S SPARE, SUBTLE STYLE, AND DELIGHT IN ITS RICHLY INTENSIFIED TOMATO FLAVOR.

3 firm, ripe tomatoes, peeled (see Note)
⅛ teaspoon salt
Pinch of freshly ground black pepper
1 clove garlic, mashed
1½ tablespoons shallots or green onions, minced
1 tablespoon fresh basil, chopped fine
1 tablespoon fresh flat-leaf parsley, chopped fine
Pinch of dried thyme
¼ cup fine white bread crumbs
⅛ cup olive oil

Preheat the oven to 400 degrees F. Cut the peeled tomatoes in half crosswise, and gently squeeze to remove the seeds and juice. Sprinkle with salt and pepper and arrange the tomatoes in a roasting pan. Do not crowd. In a small mixing bowl, combine the garlic, shallots or green onions, basil, parsley, thyme, and bread crumbs until well blended. Fill each tomato half with a spoonful or two of the bread crumb mixture, and drizzle with olive oil. (The tomatoes may be made up to this point a day ahead.) Shortly before you are ready to serve, place the tomatoes in the upper third of the preheated oven and bake for 10 to 15 minutes, or until the tomatoes are tender, but hold their shape, and the bread crumb filling has browned lightly.

MAKES 6 SERVINGS.

Note: To peel tomatoes, bring a pot of water to a rolling boil and plunge the tomatoes in the pot for several seconds until their skins crack. Remove immediately, allow to cool, and peel off skins.

Bananas Foster Flambé

ALL THE NECESSARY INGREDIENTS TO MAKE MR. CULTURE VULTURE RAPT WITH ADMIRATION, THIS DESSERT COMBINES SIMPLE INGREDIENTS WITH CULINARY TIMELESSNESS. A CLASSIC WORTH REVISITING, BANANAS FOSTER FLAMBÉ IS STUNNING. MAKE SURE YOU'VE DIMMED THE LIGHTS A BIT ON YOUR WAY OUT OF THE DINING ROOM, AND MAKE A GRAND RE-ENTRANCE. THE BRANDY SCENTED FLAMES FLUTTERING ACROSS THIS DESSERT MAKE FOR A DRAMATIC ENDING TO YOUR MEAL, AND FORESHADOW THINGS TO COME—A LITERARY OVERTURE THAT WON'T BE LOST ON YOUR MAN OF CULTURE.

½ cup butter
1 cup brown sugar
½ teaspoon cinnamon
3 ripe bananas, cut lengthwise
1 ounce brandy
Ice cream

Melt the butter and brown sugar in a medium-sized skillet or saucepan that can go from the stovetop to the table. Heat, stirring, until the sugar has dissolved. Add the bananas and toss to coat with the sugar mixture. Cook over low heat until the bananas are fully softened. In a separate small saucepan, heat the brandy, then carefully light it and pour the flaming liquid over the warm bananas. Stir occasionally until the flames disappear and serve over ice cream.

MAKES 2 SERVINGS.

CUNNING CONCOCTIONS ✴✴✴

A GUIDE TO ENTICING ELIXIRS AND SEXY LITTLE NIBBLES THAT SPEAK TO YOUR MAN. BOTTOMS UP!

THE MAN AND THE SONG	TO SIP	TO NIBBLE
MAMA'S BOY	**MINT JULEP**	**HOT CRABMEAT SOUFFLÉ**
Georgia by Ray Charles	3 ounces bourbon 6 sprigs fresh mint 1 packet of sugar Soda water *Mash mint, sugar, & Bourbon. Add soda to dissolve sugar. Fill glass with crushed ice, pour liquid through a strainer into the glass. Stir.*	8 ounces cream cheese 8 ounces lump crabmeat 1 cup imitation crab 1 clove garlic, minced ¼ cup Hellmann's mayonnaise 4 ounces Heinz horseradish sauce ½ cup scallions, chopped 1 teaspoon Dijon mustard Salt 4 tablespoons dry white wine ¼ cup sour cream Almond slivers, toasted *Heat all ingredients except crab and almonds over low heat and mix thoroughly. Fold in crabmeats. Bake in a Soufflé dish at 350 degrees F for 40 minutes or until browned. Top with toasted almonds.*

CUNNING CONCOCTIONS ✷✶✷

THE MAN AND THE SONG	TO SIP	TO NIBBLE
MR. BIG, BAD, AND RIPPLED	**BOILER MAKER**	**JALAPEÑO CHEESE SQUARES**
Tonight's the Night by Rod Stewart	2 ounces whisky with a beer chaser	1 pound Longhorn cheddar 1 pound Monterey Jack 1 4-ounce can jalapeños 2 eggs 1 can evaporated milk ½ cup flour *Grate cheese and chop jalapeños. Layer in 9-inch square pan. Mix eggs, milk, and flour and pour over cheese. Bake at 350 degrees F for 45 minutes. Cool, cut into squares, and serve*
MR. MUSIC MAN	**CALYPSO**	**VIDALIA ONION CHEESE DIP**
As Time Goes By by Frank Sinatra	2 ounces Trinidad Light Rum ½ ounce simple syrup ½ ounce orange juice 1 teaspoon lime juice *Blend in mixer with crushed ice or shake well and serve.*	1 cup chopped Vidalia onion 1 cup grated Swiss cheese 1 cup Hellmann's mayonnaise *Mix well and bake at 350 degrees F for 30 minutes. Serve.*

CUNNING CONCOCTIONS ✺✳✶

THE MAN AND THE SONG	TO SIP	TO NIBBLE
THE RUGGED OUTDOORSMAN	**BUD LIGHT**	**FROSTED PECANS**
Here Comes My Girl by Tom Petty & the Heartbreakers		1 teaspoon cold water 1 egg white 1 pound large pecans 1 teaspoon cinnamon 1 teaspoon salt 1 cup sugar *Mix water and egg white until stiff and fold in pecans. In a separate bowl, mix sugar, cinnamon, and salt. Add to pecans and mix. Spread on a greased baking sheet and bake at 225 degrees F for 1 hour. Stir occasionally.*
THE EURO-NERD	**CAMPARI & SODA WITH LIME**	**TZATZIKI**
My Funny Valentine by Chet Baker	2 ounces Campari 2 ounces soda 1 lime, quartered *Mix Campari with soda. Pour over ice. Garnish with lime.*	1 32-ounce container plain yogurt 1 large cucumber 3 garlic cloves 1½ tablespoons fresh dill 3 tablespoons olive oil 1½ tablespoons wine vinegar Salt *Drain yogurt in cheese cloth. Peel and grate cucumber. Squeeze out cucumber juice and add to yogurt. Mix in dill, oil, vinegar, and salt. Refrigerate.*

CUNNING CONCOCTIONS *

THE MAN AND THE SONG	TO SIP	TO NIBBLE
MR. MAGNATE	**BOMBAY SAPPHIRE GIN MARTINI WITH BLUE CHEESE-STUFFED OLIVES**	**BLUE CHEESE BUBBLE BREAD**
Blue Moon by Chris Isaak & The Scotty Moore Band	4 oz. Bombay Sapphire Gin 1 teaspoon dry vermouth *Fill martini shaker and martini glasses with ice and put in freezer while mixing drinks. Pour vermouth into shaker and then strain it out of shaker into chilled glass. Add gin to a shaker and shake for 30 seconds. Strain into glass and serve with blue cheese–stuffed olives.*	1 freshly baked baguette 4 ounces blue cheese, crumbled 4 ounces Hellmann's mayonnaise 1 dash Worcestershire sauce 1 teaspoon Dijon mustard *Preheat oven to 350 degrees F. Slice baguette into 1-inch slices and halve the slices. Mix cheese, mayo, Worcestershire, and mustard in a food processor until smooth. Spread mixture evenly on bread slices and bake on a cookie sheet until cheese is bubbling.*

CUNNING CONCOCTIONS ✳

THE MAN AND THE SONG	TO SIP	TO NIBBLE
THE GRILL MASTER *Come a Little Bit Closer* by Jay and the Americans	**MICHELADA** 2 cold Corona beers Juice of 2 lemons Salt *Chill 2 beer mugs. Rub rims with lemon and dip in salt. Fill each mug with juice of 1 lemon. Pour beer in glass and serve.*	**SLIDERS WITH WHITE CHEDDAR (MINI CHEESEBURGERS)** 1 pound ground beef (use an 80/20 fat ratio) ¾ teaspoon salt ½ teaspoon ground pepper 1 package dinner rolls, halved 8 small slices white cheddar Dill slices Mustard Ketchup *Mix beef, salt, and pepper together and form 2-ounce patties. Cook over medium high heat in a skillet or grill pan, turning once. Lower heat and top patties with sliced cheese. Cover pan so cheese will melt, and served on halved rolls with dill slices and condiments.*
MR. CULTURE VULTURE *You're My Thrill* by Billie Holiday	**SUGAR LIPS COCKTAIL** 2 ounces Absolut Mandarin vodka 4 ounces Fresh-squeezed orange juice 2 ounces Grand Marnier *Shake all ingredients over ice in a martini shaker and strain into sugar-rimmed, chilled martini glasses.*	**PROSCIUTTO-WRAPPED FIGS WITH STILTON CHEESE** 6 ripe Black Mission figs 6 paper-thin slices prosciutto Stilton cheese *Slice the prosciutto lengthwise into 1-inch wide strips. Clean figs with a damp towel and halve from stem end to bottom. Wrap each half with prosciutto, and arrange on a platter alongside Stilton cheese.*

CUNNING CONCOCTIONS

THE MAN AND THE SONG	TO SIP	TO NIBBLE
THE ETERNAL PEACE CORPS OFFICER *When A Man Loves a Woman* by Percy Sledge	**MOJITO** 2 ounces simple syrup 8 sprigs mint, torn 4 ounces white Bacardi rum Soda water Juice of 2 limes *Divide the simple syrup, mint, rum, and lime juice between 2 glasses and mash with the back of a spoon. Fill glasses with crushed ice and top with soda. Serve with straws, swizzle sticks and fresh mint sprigs to garnish.*	**TURKEY SAUSAGE-STUFFED MUSHROOM CAPS** 8 ounces Johnsonville or Jimmy Dean Original-style breakfast turkey sausage 8 to 10 large fresh mushroom caps *Set oven on broil with rack in highest position. Fill each mushroom cap with sausage and broil on an ovenproof platter until lightly browned. Spear each cap with toothpick to serve.*
MR. STARVING ARTIST *Painter Song* by Nora Jones	**COLORFUL POUSEE CAFE** Equal parts: Grenadine Chartreuse (yellow) Crème de Cassis Crème de Menthe (white) Chartreuse (green) Brandy *Pour carefully, in order listed, into a champagne or pousse cafe glass so that each ingredient floats on top of the previous one.* *TIP: Pour the alcohols over the back of a teaspoon to ensure that they float lightly one on top of the other.*	**PARSLEY WHITE BEAN DIP WITH PITA CHIPS** 1 can cannelloni beans, drained 2 tablespoons extra-virgin olive oil Juice of 1 lemon 2 teaspoons Dijon mustard 1 tablespoon red wine vinegar ½ cup fresh parsley leaves 2 teaspoons capers, drained Dash of cayenne pepper Sea salt Pita chips *Place all ingredients in a food processor and blend until smooth. Transfer to a serving bowl and garnish with parsley. Serve with pita chips.*

CUNNING CONCOCTIONS ✳✳✳✳

THE MAN AND THE SONG	TO SIP	TO NIBBLE
THE ALPHA MALE *My Girl* by The Temptations	**TRADITIONAL BLOODY MARY, STRAIGHT UP** 4 ounces Absolut vodka 8 ounces tomato juice 2 teaspoons horseradish 2 teaspoons Worcestershire ½ teaspoon celery salt Juice of 1 lime ½ teaspoon salt Tabasco Freshly ground black pepper *Fill 2 martini glasses with ice and place in freezer while you mix all the ingredients together in an ice-filled martini shaker. Shake vigorously. Dump ice out of the martini glasses and strain the Bloody Mary into the chilled glasses.*	**SLICED TENDERLOIN OF BEEF ON ROLLS WITH ZESTY HORSERADISH SAUCE** 2 8-ounce filet mignons, sliced into ¼-inch-thick slices 4 ounces Heinz Zesty Horseradish Sauce 2 ounces sour cream Salt Pepper 2 teaspoons olive oil 6 dinner rolls, halved horizontally *Mix horseradish sauce with sour cream and spread inside roll halves. Lightly rub filet slices with olive oil and sprinkle both sides with salt and pepper. Heat oil in skillet until hot and sear filet slices for 2 minutes on each side. Place 1 slice in each roll and serve.*

SETTING THE STAGE

GETTING THE MOOD RIGHT FOR MR. RIGHT

THE MAN	THE SETTING
THE ALPHA MALE	Think the 21 Club in New York City. The ambiance should be understated and powerful. No frills, No flowers.

- Red table linens. Red is the color of confidence, perfectly suited to the Alpha Male.

- Set a pewter water pitcher on the table in place of a glass or crystal carafe. It has a clubby, powerful presence about it.

- Use crisp, white napkins, lightly starched.

- Set opposite each other and let your man choose his seat.

- Decorate the table with two red tapers set in heavy base holders—no frilly glass or crystal.

- The plates should be simple, solid white and the silverware heavy handled and straightforward. Avoid ladies' luncheon-style china and floral silverware.

SETTING THE STAGE ✦⢁⢁

THE MAN	THE SETTING
MR. BIG, BAD, AND RIPPLED	Create a classic BBQ dinner for this man who expends lots of physical energy. The stage should be reminiscent of the laid-back picnic.

- Go for the reliable red and white–checked picnic-style table linens.

- Serve the Brunswick Stew in brown, glazed earthenware crocks.

- Present the ribs on an oval pewter or cast-iron platter set atop a wooden base.

- Cornbread should be baked in a 9-inch cast-iron skillet and go from the oven to the table.

- Decorate with a loose bouquet of yellow daisies and ivy and a few white candles.

- Set the blackberry pie out in plain view throughout the dinner.

SETTING THE STAGE ✳✱✳

THE MAN	THE SETTING
THE ETERNAL PEACE CORPS OFFICER	Transform your décor into a look that is natural, with an earthy, globe-trotting touch.

- Scent the house with a few vanilla votives.

- Buy a few yards of burlap and drape it across the table for a table cloth, or break out those batik-print placemats and napkins you've got stashed away.

- Serve the soup in a large soup bowl set on a dinner plate with the griddle cakes on the side in a white napkin-lined bread basket

- Whip butter and serve it communal style (at room temperature in a small, interesting pottery or earthenware bowl).

- Set the table with a large pepper mill and rough sea salt, the latter served in another of those interesting, small, ceramic-type bowls.

- Fill your CD player with or set your Ipod playlist to "World Music"—Putomayo CDs are in order.

SETTING THE STAGE ✳✳✳

THE MAN	THE SETTING
THE EURO-NERD	Set a small, round table for café-style dining and select your music carefully – Hotel Costes or L'Alcazar mix CDs will create the ambiance you're after. And don't dine before 8 p.m. Enjoy aperitifs and nibbles if you must invite him early.

- In lieu of open burning candles, set the table with lampshade-style candlesticks for an authentic bistro feel.

- Set the table with salt and pepper, and a specially designed mustard jar (available at specialty kitchen stores) filled with Dijon and fitted with a demitasse spoon.

- Table linens with a Provençal olive or lemon pattern are the perfect call for this man.

- Set individual butter plates with their own knives with brioche-style bread or a slice of crusty baguette.

- Consult an etiquette guide at a bookstore or library for the proper way to set the table in the style of your man's favorite European country.

SETTING THE STAGE ✦✦✦

THE MAN	THE SETTING
THE GRILL MASTER	Remember, this guy loves the flames. Make it an outdoor dinner, weather permitting, and surround yourselves with safe-burning, tiki torch-style lighting. Keep the grill within arms' reach for reassurance. ☺

- Forgo flowers and load your table with pillar candles in varying heights.

- Buy two heavy, chop house–style steak knives with serrated edges for this meal. Nothing is worse than struggling to cut good meat. Make it effortless. He'll notice.

- Set the table with a sturdy wooden pepper grinder and some fleur de sel.

- Have some oversized white napkins tied together with rope at the ready for festive bibs, and ask him which side of the T-bone he prefers.

SETTING THE STAGE ✳✦✶

THE MAN	THE SETTING
MR. MAGNATE	This man is at home in formal settings and will appreciate your efforts in creating a private-dining ambiance enhanced with luxurious, extra-special touches.

- Use pristine white table linens.

- Shine your sterling (or borrow your mother's, sister's, or best friend's), and set your table with your best antique candelabra or candlesticks. He'll notice.

- Don't save your best crystal for some "special occasion." This is it!

- Set the table with large-capacity wine goblets, a tall crystal water glass, and a silver bread bowl lined with a white linen napkin.

- Red roses are the perfect flower for this man. Cut them short and arrange them tightly in a uniform-height nosegay in a low crystal vase. Surround the arrangement with ivory-colored votives in quality votive holders.

SETTING THE STAGE ✳✴✳

THE MAN	THE SETTING
MAMA'S BOY	Is it possible to serve your meal in the kitchen or a cozy breakfast nook? If so, your Mama's Boy will be right at home. For him, the kitchen serves as the family hearth. Tie on an apron, slip into some high heels, and let him see you cook.

- Set the table so that you'll be sitting side-by-side instead of opposite each other.

- Put fresh fingertip towels and a flickering votive out on the bathroom counter.

- Use your everyday dishes with matching cloth napkins rolled into napkin rings.

- In season, cut garden flowers and greenery and arrange in an heirloom vase.

- Don't worry that you'll be tacky, offer him some ketchup with his meatloaf. The little boy in your Mama's man will say "yes."

- Offer decaf coffee or an herbal tea after dinner, and add a homey, store-bought shortbread cookie or Pepperidge Farm sweet to the saucer.

SETTING THE STAGE ✦✧

THE MAN	THE SETTING
THE MUSIC MAN	It goes without saying that you'd better have your playlist in order before this man comes dancing through your door!

- Make your table a symphony of beauty—use crisp linen placemats and napkins in the warmer months, silk ones in cooler weather.

- Whistle while you cook, and play quiet classical music while you dine.

- Forgo flowers in a vase and opt instead for an "encore look" of rose petals loosely tossed across the table.

SETTING THE STAGE ✳✲✳

THE MAN	THE SETTING
THE RUGGED OUTDOORSMAN	Entertain him where he's most at ease - at an outdoor table. And surround him with Mother Nature's best, a centerpiece composed of your area's natural treasures comprised of pinecones, pebbles, flowers, fruit, sticks, moss, or leaves.

- Use 12-by-12-inch Spanish terracotta tiles as placemats and make sure those napkin rings are wooden.

- Scour vintage stores and/or garage sales for hunting scene tableware decorated around the rims with game birds.

- Similarly, buy a couple of blue enamel camping plates at an outdoors store for serving the peach pie.

- Serve the bacon-spinach salad in individual wooden bowls.

- If you can locate it, use horn-handled silverware.

- Purchase pre-packaged "kindling" kits and be sure to have a couple of bundles of split firelogs on hand for burning. Build your fire teepee-style, posing the logs upright around the kindling and adding some lightly balled newspaper.

SETTING THE STAGE

THE MAN	THE SETTING
THE STARVING ARTIST	Ambiance is inspiration for this fellow. But he's also hungry for more affluent living. He'll notice the interesting and offbeat, and will appreciate your creativity in setting the stage.

- Instead of a full bouquet, purchase a few exotic stems such as bird of paradise, ginger, or hanging heliconia and arrange in a frog (a heavy, spiked flower holder) set atop a piece of flagstone or tile. Camouflage the frog artfully with moss or lichen.

- For fun, cover the table with brown wrapping paper and supply a tray of watercolors or a cup of pastels as part of the place setting.

- Candlelight has appeal for this man. Set the table with a couple of tapers and cover with hurricane glass for better diffusion of the light.

- Use funky platters or sushi dishes and serve your meal communal style with small individual plates for eating.

- Stemware should be unique and colorful. Consider purchasing a couple of hand-blown, colored glass goblets for the occasion.

SETTING THE STAGE *✴*

THE MAN	THE SETTING
MR. ALL-NIGHTER	It's got to be a party. Make sure the music's on, a few guests are already lounging in the living room, and the mood is festive. This man is your party animal. Keep the pace fast, and you'll keep his attention.

- You'll need the latest and trendiest décor touches and trendiest table settings. Check out your local hot spot pre-date and remember that imitation is the finest form of flattery.

- Check your stereo settings before this guy arrives. Amp up the base for the kind of background pulsing sensation he so loves.

- Consider setting a round table for added conviviality. This guy wants the action to surround him.

- He'll notice your reading materials and art on the wall. Pile a few celebrity-centered periodicals in a basket and buy or borrow a coffee table book featuring the latest photography sensation.

SETTING THE STAGE ✳

THE MAN	THE SETTING
MR. CULTURE VULTURE	Remember, this guy's been there and done that. He'll notice the subtlest of details. Avoid pop culture and streamline your look to include only the classics. No gaud, just refinement and quality.

- Set the table with starched linens and crisp-white dinner napkins. No fuss, just straight-forward class.

- Avoid cut glass crystal and if need be, purchase tasting-quality wine glasses for the occasion. Reidel is an excellent choice.

- Set a water glass and wine glasses appropriate to your vintage of choice.

- Break out the linen fingertip towels for the bathroom, and don't forget a fresh bar of French-milled, hand-cut soap.

- Keep the dinner music hushed and classical, or forgo it altogether.

- He'll likely come armed with flowers and/or wine. Arrange the blooms on the spot in a clear glass or crystal vase, and put either gift on the table immediately.

- If your dinnerware is flowery or heavy, borrow or buy something simple and chic. A simple, silver-rimmed white plate will make him feel at home.

part 2

In the Mood

So you've snagged him – at least for a few hours. Bravo! Now what? You can't afford to fumble. Take stock of your situation—what's the occasion? Then flip to our custom-made menus for guidance. The recipes in this section were created with *carpe diem* in mind; they speak to the moment, placing time firmly on your side. You'll whet his appetite with your culinary talents, and by mid-meal, he'll be doing exactly what it is *you* want.

In the following pages you'll find menus with a minimum of three courses and an accompanying song and a beverage for the myriad occasions you and your man might face. Follow these meal suggestions, and you'll get the mood right, no matter what type of man you've invited over. Face that first morning after with confidence by whipping up a batch of tiny melt-in-your-mouth muffins and a fluffy, bright, Zucchini Frittata. Capture that commitment with cool, collected Vichyssoise and a luxurious Dover Sole with White Grapes. Or send him packing with a Dear John dinner of Chilled Cucumber Soup, Cold Chinese Noodles, and Lemon Ice.

Don't forget to Set Your Stage for romance by following the atmosphere-enhancing steps outlined in our handy chart at section's end. That little black dress and a single strand of choker-length pearls will Capture That Commitment, Ylang Ylang and rose petals will enhance your aphrodisiac evening, and sparklers should be on hand when its time for Let's Celebrate. And even if a full meal is not on the agenda, live for the moment with our easy-to-assemble cocktail and appetizer ideas contained in the Cunning Concoctions chart also found after the menus.

The aim of this section is to stack the deck in your favor. It's the moment you've been waiting for, just the right time to make your move. Don't let romance elude you. Get on out there and take advantage of your situation. These are meals designed to put you in the driver's seat. Your destiny is of your own creating. Rev up your engine, and get cooking!

Chapter 13
Aphrodisiacs 101

Manipulation at its finest! This menu gets blood pumping, pulses quickening, heads rushing, bodies flushing, hands traveling, and juices flowing. Begin with Scallops Ceviche, a "raw" food treat as invigorating as it is cool and refreshing. Then move to the classic libido-enhancing Oysters on the Half Shell enlivened with a punchy Pink Peppercorn Vinaigrette. Fried Lobster Fingers make for enticing finger food—absolute digit-licking luxury! Finally, let's hope dessert goes to his head. It's a sparingly sweet, seductively flirtatious Champagne Sorbet designed to bring out the best in him.

THE SONG: *Fever* by Peggy Lee

THE BEVERAGE: Chevalier Montrachet White Bordeaux, slightly chilled

Scallops Ceviche

A COOL, COME-HITHER MENU OPENER, THESE SCALLOPS TANTALIZE THE SENSES WITH A HEALTHY DOSE OF ENERGIZING CITRUS AND BRIGHT COLOR. THEY WILL HAVE YOU BOTH FLUSHING IN ANTICIPATION OF WHAT'S TO COME. CEVICHE OFFERS SUSTENANCE, BUT WON'T SATE YOUR APPETITE OR LEAVE YOU FEELING HEAVY AND DULL.

2 pounds bay scallops
Juice of 12 limes (or enough juice to submerge scallops completely)
2 cloves garlic, minced
¼ cup scallions, chopped
½ cup green bell pepper, chopped
½ cup red bell pepper, chopped
¼ cup parsley, chopped
¼ cup cilantro, chopped
¼ cup shallots, chopped
1 teaspoon mustard seed
1½ teaspoon salt
2 dashes Tabasco
½ cup olive oil
Salad greens for presentation

Pour the lime juice over the scallops and refrigerate for 3 to 4 hours. Drain, leaving a little juice, then toss the scallops with the garlic, scallions, bell peppers, parsley, cilantro, shallots, mustard seed, salt, and Tabasco. Mix well. Add the olive oil and stir well to coat. Refrigerate for an additional hour. Line a serving bowl with salad greens and fill with the scallop mixture.

MAKES 4 SERVINGS.

Oysters on the Half Shell with Pink Peppercorn Mignonnette

ALTHOUGH THIS RECIPE SHOULD BE MADE FROM THE FRESHEST OYSTERS AVAILABLE IN YOUR AREA, LOOK FOR (OR ASK YOUR FISH MONGER TO ORDER) APPALACHICOLA OYSTERS. THEY ARE FROM THE GULF AREA OF FLORIDA, AND ARE A FAVORITE FOR THEIR NATURAL SALTY OCEAN FLAVOR AND SIZE. PLAN ON 12 OYSTERS FOR EACH OF YOU. IF YOU HAVE NOT SHUCKED AN OYSTER BEFORE, ASK A PROFESSIONAL TO DO IT FOR YOU. OR BRING THEM HOME IN THE SHELL AND PUT YOUR MAN TO THE TEST. HE LIKES TO BE CALLED ON FOR MANLY DUTIES!

24 raw Appalachicola oysters on the half-shell, chilled, with shell "liquor" reserved
1 lemon cut into wedge

Pink Peppercorn Mignonnette

MIGNONNETTE LOOSELY TRANSLATES AS "CUTE LITTLE THING," AND THIS VINAIGRETTE MAKES A MORE CHARMING ACCOMPANIMENT TO OYSTERS THAN THICK, FIERY COCKTAIL SAUCE. SCINTILLATING AND TART, IT IS A MATCH MADE IN HEAVEN.

1 tablespoon pink peppercorns, crushed
¼ cup red wine vinegar
1 shallot, minced fine
¼ pear, minced fine
¼ teaspoon coarsely ground black pepper

In a small mixing bowl, whisk together the peppercorns, vinegar, shallot, pear bits, and pepper, and let stand at room temperature for 30 minutes. Arrange the oysters on crushed ice around the periphery of two large round plates. Place a small dip bowl in the center of each oyster plate and fill with the Mignonnette. Garnish the plates with fresh lemon wedges.

MAKES 2 SERVINGS.

Fried Lobster Fingers with Honey-Dijon Sauce

AN ENTICING TAKE ON A SURE-FIRE APHRODISIAC, THIS RECIPE TURNS LOBSTER INTO MANAGE-ABLE FINGER FOOD. THE HONEY-DIJON SAUCE IS A SWEET FOIL FOR THIS KING OF CRUS-TACEANS—DIP, AND SUCK TO YOUR HEART (AND BODY'S) CONTENT!

4 8-ounce cold-water lobster tails
4 cups vegetable oil
1 egg, beaten
1¼ cup unseasoned bread crumbs
½ teaspoon dry mustard
1½ tablespoons Dijon mustard
⅓ cup honey

With a sharp knife, split the lobster tails lengthwise to make "fingers." In a deep frying pan, heat the oil to 350 degrees F. Dip the lobster fingers in the egg and then in the bread crumbs. Carefully set the fingers into the hot oil and fry until golden brown. Drain on a paper towel. Meanwhile, mix the dry mustard with the Dijon until well incorporated. Add the honey and stir to blend. Drizzle over the lobster fingers and serve.

MAKES 2 SERVINGS.

Champagne Sorbet

KEEP THE SENSES STIRRING WITH THIS DESSERT OF FROZEN BUBBLY. CHAMPAGNE CREATES AMBIANCE LIKE NO OTHER BEVERAGE, AND PROVIDES THE PERFECT PUNCTUATION TO YOUR APHRODISIAC MEAL. POP A BOTTLE OF CHILLED CHAMPAGNE TO SIP WITH YOUR SPOONFULS OF SORBET. YOUR DECADENCE WILL BE WELL REWARDED.

5 cups sugar
4¼ cups water
1⅔ cups champagne
⅔ cup non-effervescent mineral water
Juice of 1 lemon or juice of half an orange

Combine the sugar and water in a saucepan set over high heat, stirring continuously until the sugar has dissolved. Continue heating until the mixture comes to a boil. Immediately remove the syrup from the saucepan and pour it into a large bowl or jar and refrigerate. Once cooled thoroughly, add the champagne, mineral water, and juice and process in an ice cream machine according to manufacturer's instructions.

MAKES 1 QUART.

Chapter 14
Capture That Commitment

Parting won't ever occur to him after sharing this rock-solid meal with you. A sublime marriage of the strong and scintillating, this menu lays a firm foundation. Ease into your new permanence with a cool classic. Vichyssoise comes on soft and gentle, its coolness disguising its affirmed, "stick-to-you" leek-and-potato base. Your new status as a couple deserves feting, and Dover Sole with White Grapes is a delicacy—celebration food at its finest. Tiny Carrot Timbales drive home the message, elevating an otherwise humble root vegetable to the unforgettable. Finally, close the deal with the irresistible—a Chocolate Soufflé as rich and delicious as your union is sure to be.

Vichyssoise

VICHYSSOISE IS COOL AND COLLECTED, A MIRROR IMAGE OF YOU IN THE FACE OF YOUR NEW UNION. THIS REASSURING SOUP HAILS FROM FRANCE, A LAND WHERE LOVING IS SAID TO BE THE NATIONAL PASTIME. FULL OF SMOOTH MOVES, IT'LL HAVE YOU LOCKING LIPS IN NO TIME, SEALING YOUR COMMITMENT WITH A KISS!

2 tablespoons butter
5 leeks, white part only, cut into rounds
1 medium onion, sliced
4 potatoes, peeled and sliced thin
Salt
White pepper
4 cups chicken stock
2 cups milk
2½ cups half and half
Juice of half a lemon
Fresh chives, chopped fine

In a large saucepan, melt the butter and add the leeks and onions, cooking over medium heat until tender but not brown. Stir frequently. Add the potatoes, salt, and white pepper to taste, and the chicken stock. Bring to a boil and simmer for 20 minutes or until the potatoes are tender. Puree the mixture in a food processor and return it to the saucepan. Stir in the milk and half and half. Taste, and add lemon juice for seasoning. Chill soup until ready to serve. Garnish with chopped fresh chives.

MAKES 8 SERVINGS.

Baked Dover Sole with White Grapes

½ pound fresh Dover sole (2¼-pound fillets)
½ cup mayonnaise (preferably Hellmann's)
½ cup sour cream
Juice of 1 lemon
½ cup seedless green grapes
Freshly ground nutmeg

Preheat the oven to 350 degrees F. Butter a glass baking dish and layer the sole fillets in the bottom of the dish. In a small mixing bowl, combine the mayonnaise, sour cream, and lemon juice. Spread the mixture over the sole and place the grapes over the top. Sprinkle with freshly ground nutmeg. Bake for 25 minutes and serve immediately.

MAKES 2 SERVINGS.

Creamy Carrot Timbales

SWEET AND SMOOTH, YET STURDY—THIS IS THE WAY TO EAT CARROTS! DELIGHTFUL LITTLE "FLANS" OF THIS BETA CAROTENE–RICH ROOT VEGGIE BECKON PRETTILY FROM THE PLATE AND PROVIDE AN OUT-OF-THE-ORDINARY TOUCH TO YOUR CELEBRATORY DINNER. THESE TIMBALES REQUIRE A LITTLE EXTRA WORK ON YOUR PART, BUT YOUR EFFORTS WILL BE WELL REWARDED.

1 large carrot
Salt
1 pound carrots, sliced thin
3 tablespoons all-purpose flour
4 eggs
1 cup whipping cream
³/₄ teaspoon salt
¹/₂ teaspoon freshly ground white pepper
Freshly grated nutmeg

Preheat the oven to 375 degrees F. Butter the bottom and sides of six 1/2-cup-size timbale molds (miniature soufflé dishes). Line each cup with a circle of waxed paper, and butter the paper. Cut the thickest part of the large carrot into six rounds, and scallop the edges of the rounds to resemble a flower. Boil water in a medium sauce-pan and add a pinch of salt. When the water is at a rolling boil, add the scalloped carrot rounds and cook for several minutes or until just tender. Remove with a slotted spoon and drain well. Do not remove the water from heat. Place one scalloped carrot round in the bottom of each timbale mold. Add the sliced carrots to the boiling water and cook until tender. Drain well and puree the carrots in a food processor or blender until smooth. Transfer the puree to a mixing bowl and sprinkle with the flour. In a separate mixing bowl, beat the eggs with the whipping cream until thick. Add the salt, pepper, and freshly grated nutmeg to taste and mix well. Add to the pureed carrot mixture and blend well. Divide the mixture evenly between the timbale molds and cover each with a round of buttered waxed paper. Place the timbales in a shal-low baking dish and pour boiling water into the dish to fill halfway up the sides of the timbale molds. Bake until set, approximately 30 minutes. Remove molds from water, discard waxed paper, and let stand 5 minutes. Once slightly cooled, run the tip of a sharp knife around the edge of the mold to loosen the timbales. Invert three timbales onto each plate to serve and discard the waxed paper.

MAKES 6 SERVINGS.

Chocolate Soufflé

THIS IS A SWEET THAT WILL SEAL YOUR COMMITMENT WITH THE FIRST SPOONFUL. POSITIVELY IRRESISTIBLE, IT IS LUSCIOUSLY LIGHT, YET PACKED WITH RICH, CHOCOLATE FLAVOR AND A HINT OF MOCHA. ALTHOUGH THIS SOUFFLÉ EXITS THE OVEN MAJESTIC ENOUGH TO SERVE EIGHT, YOU AND YOUR MAN WILL LIKELY FIND IT HARD TO STOP SAVORING IT AS A DUO. GO AHEAD AND INDULGE—YOU OWE IT TO EACH OTHER.

2 squares semisweet baking chocolate
3 tablespoons coffee
3 tablespoons butter
3 tablespoons flour
1 cup milk
½ cup sugar
¼ teaspoon salt
4 egg yolks, lightly beaten
5 egg whites, beaten until stiff

In the top of a double boiler set over low heat, melt the chocolate squares in the coffee and set aside. In a separate saucepan set over medium-low heat, melt the butter and stir in the flour. Gradually add the milk, stirring constantly. Add the sugar and salt, and stir until well incorporated. Transfer the melted chocolate to the butter mixture and continue stirring. When the sauce is thick and smooth, remove the pan from the heat and allow the sauce to cool. Preheat the oven to 400 degrees F. When the chocolate sauce has cooled, add the egg yolks and beat well. Gently fold in the stiff egg whites. Butter a 5- to 6-cup soufflé dish and sprinkle it with sugar. Carefully transfer the soufflé batter to the dish, and set the dish in a shallow pan of hot, but not boiling, water. Bake in a preheated 400 degree F oven for 5 minutes. Reduce the oven temperature to 375 degrees F and continue baking for an additional 25 to 30 minutes or until set.

MAKES 6 SERVINGS.

Chapter 15
Let's Celebrate

The mood is light and festive, with a menu made to match. Keep it bright and lively with this dazzling repast. Corn Chowder finds an otherwise humble starch all dressed up and dandy, swathed in a creamy cloak fit for a party. Live Maine Lobster screams "special occasion." Regale your guests with these luxurious crustaceans dabbed with a glistening Beurre Blanc, and nestle the lobsters next to a pretty side of Sugar Snap Peas sautéed with a confetti of red and yellow bell pepper. Nothing says "celebration!" better than sparkling wine. Pour flutes of Spanish Cava to accompany this frothy, elegant, champagne-based dessert riddled with fresh berries, and you'll double your fun for sure.

THE SONG: *Steppin' Out with My Baby* by Fred Astaire

THE BEVERAGE: Sparkling Spanish Cava

Corn Chowder

EARTHY CORN GETS ELEVATED TO ELEGANT PARTY FOOD IN THIS DELECTABLY CREAMY SOUP SMOLDERING WITH THE SLIGHTEST HINT OF SMOKY BACON. MAKE THIS SOUP AHEAD OF TIME AND SERVE IT, GARNISHED WITH FRESH PARSLEY, FROM A STARK, WHITE TERRINE. THIS ISN'T THE STUFF OF DELICATE SIPPING. IT IS BOLD AND BRIGHT—A VERITABLE GALA OF FLAVOR PACKED INTO EVERY SPOONFUL.

1 pound bacon, cut into ½-inch pieces
3 tablespoons flour
1 small onion, chopped fine
1 cup celery, diced
2 cups potatoes, diced
1 cup carrots, diced
1 quart milk
1 16-ounce can creamed corn
2 teaspoons salt
½ teaspoon white pepper
1 teaspoon Worcestershire sauce
Fresh parsley, chopped, for garnish

Fry the bacon, reserving 2 tablespoons of drippings. Add the flour to the bacon and the reserved drippings and stir to combine. Remove from heat. In a separate saucepan, combine the onion, celery, potatoes, and carrots and just cover with water. Bring to a boil and cook for 10 minutes or until the vegetables are tender. Add the bacon mixture to the vegetables, stir, and cook for an additional 10 minutes. Stir in the milk, corn, salt, pepper, and Worcestershire sauce and bring to a boil again. Immediately reduce heat to low and cook until ready to serve. Serve garnished with fresh, chopped parsley.

MAKES 8 SERVINGS.

Boiled Live Maine Lobster

A FAVORITE OF THE RICH AND FAMOUS, BOILED LOBSTER IS A CULINARY STUNNER IN SPITE OF ITS SIMPLICITY. TIMING IS EVERYTHING WHEN IT COMES TO LOBSTER'S PREPARATION. DON'T OVER-COOK IT OR YOU'LL END UP WITH A RUBBERY REPLACEMENT FOR WHAT OTHERWISE QUALIFIES AS FOOD FOR THE GODS. SERVE ON A LARGE WHITE OR STERLING SILVER PLATTER SURROUNDED BY LEMONS, AND BE PREPARED FOR PLENTY OF OOHS AND AAHS FROM YOUR MAN!

2 1½-pound live Maine lobsters
3 lemons
Salt for boiling water

Fill a large stockpot with water, enough to cover the lobsters entirely once added, and bring to a boil. For each quart of water used, add 1 heaping tablespoon of salt. When the water is at a rolling boil, slide the lobsters head first into the pot. When the water returns to a boil, reduce the heat to medium-low and simmer for 7 min-utes. (If the lobsters' shells are soft to the touch prior to boiling, reduce the simmer-ing time by a minute per pound.) Drain and serve with Beurre Blanc (recipe follows).

MAKES 2 SERVINGS.

Beurre Blanc

A DELICACY SERVED IN THE OPULENT BANQUET HALLS OF THE FRENCH COURT, THIS SAUCE IS THE CADILLAC OF BLENDED BUTTERS! WHEN PREPARING THE BEURRE BLANC, BE VERY CAREFUL TO KEEP THE PAN AT MEDIUM TO LOW HEAT. IF THE BUTTER GETS TOO HOT, THE MIXTURE WILL SEPARATE.

1 small shallot, chopped fine
3 tablespoons white wine vinegar
3 tablespoons white wine
¾ cup cold, salted butter, cut into small pieces
Salt
White pepper, ground fine

In the top of a double boiler set over high heat, boil the shallot in the vinegar and wine until the mixture has reduced to approximately 1 tablespoon. Reduce the heat to low (water in bottom of double boiler should be simmering, not boiling). Gradually whisk in the butter piece by piece until all of it is well incorporated. Season with salt and white pepper to taste. Serve immediately.

MAKES 3/4 CUP.

Sautéed Sugar Snap Peas with Sweet Bell Pepper

EASY TO PREPARE AND PRETTY ON THE PLATE, THIS FRESH VEGETABLE SAUTÉ IS A FESTIVE ACCOMPANIMENT TO THE RICHLY SAUCED LOBSTER AND THICK, SMOKY SOUP. FOR ADDED PERK, SNIP SOME FRESH CHIVES OVER THE TOP BEFORE SERVING.

5 tablespoons butter
1½ pounds sugar snap peas, strings removed
Half a red bell pepper, cut into ½-inch cubes
Half a yellow bell pepper, cut into ½-inch cubes
½ teaspoon sugar
Salt
Pepper

Melt the butter in a large skillet set over high heat. Add the peas and bell peppers and sauté until tender, approximately 3 to 4 minutes. Sprinkle with sugar and toss to coat evenly. Season to taste with salt and pepper and serve hot.

MAKES 6 SERVINGS.

Champagne Sabayon with Fresh Berries

YOU'LL BE TOASTED AGAIN AND AGAIN FOR THIS REFRESHING ENDING TO YOUR STAR-STUDDED MEAL. THE PERFECT DESSERT ON THE HEELS OF LOBSTER, CHAMPAGNE SABAYON IS A LUXURI-OUSLY FROTHY INDULGENCE. THE FRESH BERRIES MAKE IT BEAUTIFUL. SERVE THE SABAYON IN CURVACEOUS PARFAIT GLASSES OR TALL, SLIM FLUTES ALONGSIDE A GLASS OF FRESHLY UNCORKED BUBBLY FOR A DOUBLE DOSE OF CELEBRATION. (NOTE: NEVER MAKE SABAYON FROM INFERIOR QUALITY CHAMPAGNE. YOUR RESULTS WILL GO FROM TANTALIZING TO UNREMARKABLE.)

4 egg yolks
$1/3$ cup granulated sugar
$3/4$ cup champagne
2 tablespoons Kirsch (cherry liqueur)
4 cups assorted fresh berries

Fill the bottom pan of a double boiler with water and bring to a boil over high heat. In the top of the double broiler, whisk together the egg yolks and sugar and stir until foamy. Add the champagne and continue whisking constantly, until the mixture thickens into a light cream, approximately 10 minutes. Remove the pan from heat and stir in the Kirsch. Spoon the mixture over the assorted fresh berries and serve immediately.

MAKES 4 SERVINGS.

Chapter 16
The "Dear John" Dinner

Better than a letter, this dinner is the kitchen's answer to the cold shower. Things have gone limp and icy between you, as frigid as a bowl of Chilled Cucumber Soup, and there's no looking up. A tangled bowl of Cold Chinese Noodles speaks volumes about where you are with your relationship. It's messy and frigid; its spice tamed, its flavor mild. Face it, things have soured, but you don't want to end it on a bitter note. Lemon Ice sends your message, yet keeps its tone bright, signifying your hope that closing this door means the possibility of opening another.

THE SONG: *You Can't Always Get What You Want* by The Rolling Stones

THE BEVERAGE: Chilled Sake in a wooden sake box

Chilled Cucumber Soup

HE'LL BE GREEN WITH ENVY THAT YOU'RE MOVING ON AS HE SIPS THIS MILD-MANNERED SOUP. IT MAY HAVE BEEN CREATED TO SEND HIM PACKING, BUT IT STILL TASTES AND FEELS REFRESHING. IT'S A STRAIGHTFORWARD MEAL STARTER—AS FRANK AND UNCOMPLICATED AS YOUR INTENTION TO CALL IT QUITS.

3 medium cucumbers, peeled, seeded, and chopped
3 tablespoons green bell pepper, chopped (about ½ pepper)
2 cups chicken stock
1 cup sour cream
1 teaspoon salt
2 teaspoons fresh dill, chopped
Fresh dill sprigs for garnish

Combine the cucumbers, bell pepper, chicken stock, sour cream, salt, and chopped dill in a blender and puree until smooth. Chill until ready to serve. Garnish with a sprig of fresh dill.

MAKES 4 SERVINGS.

Cold Chinese Noodles

FLACCID AND FRIGID, THESE NOODLES ARE AS TANGLED AND CONFUSED AS YOUR PARTNERSHIP. THE FIRE IS GONE. THE ZIP EXTINGUISHED. WHAT YOU'RE LEFT WITH IS COLD SILENCE AS YOU IDLY TWIRL YOUR FORKS, LOST IN THOUGHTS OF BETTER DAYS.

1 pre-cooked boneless, skinless whole chicken breast, cut into thin strips
5 ounces boiled or baked ham, sliced and cut into thin strips
1 bunch scallions (including green tops) cut into 2-inch lengths, then halved
    lengthwise
½ cup walnuts, coarsely chopped
1 pound rice vermicelli or Chinese rice stick noodles, cooked, drained, and cooled
1½ cups vegetable oil
2½ tablespoons light sesame oil
2 tablespoons ground coriander seeds
¾ cup soy sauce
1 teaspoon hot chili oil (optional)

Combine chicken, ham, scallions, and walnuts in a large mixing bowl. Add the cooked noodles, stir, and set aside. Heat the vegetable and sesame oils in a small saucepan over medium heat. Remove the pan from heat and stir in the coriander seeds and soy sauce. (Stand back when doing this; the mixture will sizzle and splatter.) Add the chili oil if desired, and blend well. Pour the hot dressing over the noodles and toss to coat evenly. Transfer the noodles to a large serving bowl, toss again to distribute dressing, and refrigerate until cold, approximately 3 hours.

MAKES 6 SERVINGS.

Lemon Ice

LIGHT AND TANTALIZING—THE BREATH OF FRESH AIR YOU BOTH SEEK—THIS TART DESSERT CON-CLUDES THINGS ONCE AND FOR ALL. YOUR DEAL HAS GONE SOUR, BUT THIS REFRESHING ENDING IS A REMINDER THAT BOTH YOUR FUTURES ARE BRIGHT.

2 cups sugar
1 cup water
1 cup lemon juice
1 cup ice cubes
1 tablespoon finely grated lemon zest
Lemon zest for garnish
Fresh mint sprigs for garnish

Combine the sugar and the water in a 1-quart saucepan. Bring to a boil over medium heat, stirring constantly. Once the sugar has dissolved completely, cool the syrup to room temperature. Add the lemon juice, ice, and zest, and stir until all the ice has melted. Pour the mixture into two metal freezer trays. When the ice has frozen nearly solid, remove from the freezer and chop it in a blender until slushy. Serve in champagne flutes or parfait glasses garnished with lemon zest and fresh mint.

MAKES 6 SERVINGS.

Chapter 17
The Morning After

Charge boldly into the new day, leaving no room for regrets. This menu ensures a repeat performance, reminding him he can never get too much of a good thing—plus, it will prevent you from rummaging around unromantically in the refrigerator's unflattering light for post-sex sustenance! Take the *toro* by the horns and greet the day with a feisty Bloody Bull. Beefy and spicy, it's a macho beginning that will have him roaring. The tiny muffin biscuits that follow may be small, but they're big on flavor—flirtatious little mouthfuls he'll love to nibble. The Zucchini Frittata will require you to get out of bed and into the kitchen. But it's for a good cause—warming sustenance for both of you, so you can enjoy a Take 2 once you've cleared the dishes.

THE SONG: *What a Wonderful World* by Louis Armstrong

THE BEVERAGE: Fresh-squeezed OJ and/or the Bloody Bull

Bloody Bull

THIS BLOODY MARY REVISITED IS THICK AND ENERGIZING, A PROTEIN- AND VITAMIN-PACKED LIBIDO ENHANCER DESIGNED TO GET YOU AND YOUR MAN UP AND MOVING. TO EASE INTO YOUR MORNING, MAKE THIS STOUT MIXER THE NIGHT BEFORE AND ADD THE EYE-OPENING SHOT OF VODKA THE MORNING AFTER. SLIDE ONE OF THESE INTO HIS HAND AS YOU SLIP OUT OF THE BEDROOM AND INTO THE KITCHEN; HE'LL BE READY FOR A LITTLE ROUGHHOUSING WHEN YOU RETURN. *OLÉ!*

4 ounces vodka
4 ounces beef consommé, preferably Campbell's
8 ounces Bloody Mary mix, preferably Tabasco brand
1 teaspoon prepared horseradish
1 teaspoon Worcestershire sauce
1/2 teaspoon celery salt
Coarsely ground fresh black pepper
Pepperoncini and large, green, pimiento-stuffed olives for garnish

Place two ice-filled martini glasses in the freezer while you prepare your drink mix. Mix vodka, consommé, Bloody Mary mix, horseradish, Worcestershire sauce, celery salt, and several ice cubes in a cocktail shaker and shake to blend and chill. Remove the martini glasses from the freezer and discard the ice. Pour in Bloody Bull and garnish with pepperoncini and olives.

MAKES 2 SERVINGS.

Tiny Muffin Biscuits

THEY LOOK LIKE LITTLE MUFFINS BUT ARE ACTUALLY MINI BISCUITS—TINY BITES OF MORNING DELIGHT. SERVE THEM IN THE BEDROOM. THEIR DIMINUTIVE SIZE MAKES THEM THE IDEAL NO-MESS, BREAKFAST-IN-BED TREAT.

2 cups biscuit mix, such as Bisquick
1 stick butter, melted and cooled
1 ounce sour cream

Preheat the oven to 425 degrees F. In a small bowl, mix together the biscuit mix, melted butter, and sour cream until smooth. Drop tablespoon by tablespoon into a greased or non-stick mini muffin tin. Bake on the center oven rack for approximately 15 minutes or until golden.

MAKES 2 SERVINGS.

Zucchini Frittata

THIS EGG DISH IS WORTH ROLLING OUT OF BED FOR. YOUR MAN WILL MISS YOU WHILE YOU'RE GONE, BUT ABSENCE MAKES THE HEART GROW FONDER. HE'LL BE SO IMPRESSED WITH THIS EGGY, CHEESY, BRIGHTLY SEASONED PIE, STAYING THE NIGHT WILL BECOME HABIT-FORMING. DON'T LET THE LENGTHY INGREDIENT LIST DETER YOU, THIS FRITTATA COMES TOGETHER IN A DASH AND OUTDOES UNINSPIRING TOASTER WAFFLES BY A LONG SHOT.

2 to 3 tablespoons butter or extra-virgin olive oil
1½ cups onion, chopped
½ pound zucchini, peeled and shredded
12 eggs, beaten
2 tablespoons fresh basil (or 2 teaspoons dried basil)
2 teaspoons salt
Cracked black pepper
3 tablespoons dry bread crumbs
2 cloves garlic, minced
2 tomatoes, peeled and sliced
1 cup grated cheddar cheese
½ cup grated Parmesan cheese

Preheat the oven to 350 degrees F. Heat the butter or olive oil in a skillet set over high heat. Add the onion and sauté until translucent. Add the zucchini and cook, stirring, for approximately 2 minutes. Remove from heat and allow to cool. In a large mixing bowl, beat the eggs and add the basil, salt, and pepper. Transfer the onion-zucchini mixture to the eggs and stir well. Add the bread crumbs and garlic, and mix well. Pour into a buttered quiche dish or pie pan and arrange the sliced tomatoes on top. Sprinkle with the cheddar and Parmesan cheeses, and bake for 20 to 25 minutes or until set.

MAKES 6 SERVINGS.

Chapter 18
Pure Seduction

He'll be putty in your hands before you know it with this menu. Smooth, creamy, rich . . . in a word: irresistible! Blinis and caviar are undeniably sexy. In this menu, supremely refined caviar stands as a bold symbol of fertility, and is made all the more enticing as it glistens atop pliant blinis kissed with the sweetness of corn. Salmon Wellington stars as the main course. It is creamy and inviting, wonderful for spoon-feeding your object of desire. Pull out all the stops by plying your man with homemade chocolate truffles at meal's end and beyond. Dense, unctuous, and unbelievably addictive, they offer a high that will send you soaring right into each other's arms.

THE SONG: *Your Love Is King* by Sade
THE BEVERAGE: Veuve Clicquot Orange Label Champagne

Corn Blinis with Crème Fraîche and Caviar

CAVIAR BECKONS LUSTILY FROM ITS PERCH ATOP THESE DELICATE CORN BLINIS. THE PERFECT FOIL FOR CAVIAR, BLINIS ARE A RUSSIAN TREAT—A LIGHTER, AIRIER PANCAKE, PERFECT AS A PASSED HORS D'OEUVRE PRE-DINNER. THESE DELIGHTFUL LITTLE DISCS OFFER A HINT OF CORN FLAVOR, BUT REMAIN SUBTLE IN ORDER TO ALLOW THE CAVIAR TO SHINE. PURCHASE THE HIGHEST QUALITY CAVIAR YOU CAN AFFORD, AND GO EASY ON THE CRÈME FRAÎCHE. IT'S SO SMOOTH AND DELICIOUS YOU'LL BE TEMPTED TO USE IT GENEROUSLY.

1½ cup fresh corn kernels, about 2 ears
½ cup milk
⅓ cup cornmeal
⅓ cup flour
4 tablespoons butter, melted
2 eggs
2 egg yolks
½ teaspoon salt
½ teaspoon pepper
¼ cup fresh chives, chopped fine
½ cup clarified butter (see Note)
Crème fraîche (recipe follows)
Assorted caviars (oestra, sevruga, golden whitefish, salmon roe, and beluga)

Roughly chop the corn kernels or process in short bursts in a food processor until a chunky, slightly creamy texture is achieved. In a large mixing bowl, blend together the corn, milk, cornmeal, and flour, whisking until entirely smooth. In a separate bowl, whisk together the melted butter, whole eggs, and egg yolks. Once blended, stir the egg mixture into the corn mixture and season with salt, pepper, and half of the chives. Heat a large skillet over high heat and add the clarified butter. Once hot, pour the batter in silver dollar–size doses into the pan, and cook for 2 minutes on each side or until golden brown. Serve topped with a dollop of crème fraîche (recipe follows) and caviar. Garnish with the remaining chives.

Note: *Clarified butter is made by melting butter and separating the transparent, golden butter from the heavier milk solids, which cause the butter to burn easily. To separate, skim the foam from the top of the warmed melted butter, then pour off the clear liquid into a separate container carefully so as not to disturb the heavier solids that will accumulate at the bottom of the pan.*

MAKES 30 BLINIS.

Crème Fraîche

LIP-SMACKING LUXURY, CRÈME FRAÎCHE RAISES THE BAR ON ORDINARY SOUR CREAM AND INVITES INDULGENCE. KEEP A BATCH IN THE FRIDGE FOR IMPROMPTU SAUCING.

1 cup heavy cream (not ultra-pasteurized)
1 cup sour cream

Whisk the heavy cream and sour cream together in a bowl. Cover loosely with plastic wrap and let the mixture stand at room temperature overnight, or until thickened. (In cooler climes, this may take as long as 24 hours.) Cover and refrigerate for at least 4 hours. The mixture will continue to thicken. Serve with savory or sweet preparations.

MAKES 2 CUPS.

Salmon Wellington

SALMON'S OMEGA-3 RICH FLESH HAS BEEN TOUTED AS A FOUNTAIN OF YOUTH, AND THIS ENTRÉE IS AS BRIGHT AND VIGOROUS AS YOUNG MAN IN HIS SEXUAL PRIME. A TAKE ON THE BEEF DISH OF THE SAME NAME, THIS SALMON VERSION OOZES GOOD TASTE WITH DEVILISH INTENTIONS. IT'S A SEDUCTIVE STUDY IN CONTRADICTION YOUR MAN WON'T BE ABLE TO IGNORE. SPOON-FEED HIM BY CANDLELIGHT AND THE NIGHT WILL BE YOURS.

1 can black beans, drained
2 pounds boneless salmon filets, skin removed
Juice of ½ lemon
6 ounces whole fresh mushrooms
1 bunch fresh baby spinach
½ ounce pink peppercorns, crushed
2 unbaked puff pastry sheets, preferably Pepperidge Farm brand
1 egg, lightly beaten

Preheat the oven to 400 degrees F. Spray a baking sheet with cooking spray and set aside. In a blender or food processor, puree the drained black beans until smooth. Wash and dry the salmon filets, cover with the lemon juice, and set aside. Separate the mushroom caps and stems, setting the caps aside. Chop the spinach and mushroom stems coarsely and toss together with the peppercorns. Spread the pureed black beans on one side of each pastry sheet, leaving a 1-inch margin on all sides. Place one pastry sheet, bean side up, on a baking sheet. Make a nest in the center of the sheet with the spinach/mushroom mixture. Place the salmon filets on the spinach and arrange the mushroom caps across the top. Cover with the remaining pastry sheet, bean side down. Crimp the edges to seal and trim excess pastry, using left-over strips to decorate the top of the pastry. Brush the pastry with the egg and make several small slits across the top of the dough. Bake for 20 minutes or until golden brown.

MAKES 4 SERVINGS.

Chocolate Truffles

HOMEMADE AND HEAVENLY, THESE TRUFFLES WILL PROVE THAT STORE-BOUGHT CHOCOLATES JUST AREN'T UP TO PAR. THESE BALLS OF PLEASURE ARE SURPRISINGLY EASY TO MAKE, AND WELL WORTH THE DO-AHEAD EFFORT. HAND FEED YOUR MAN, AND HE'LL THANK YOU WITH A SEDUCTION GAME BEYOND YOUR WILDEST DREAMS.

1 pound semisweet chocolate
5 egg yolks
2 cups confectioner's sugar
1 cup butter, at room temperature
5 tablespoons sour cream
5 tablespoons brandy
1 cup quality cocoa powder

Melt the chocolate in the top of a double boiler. In a separate mixing bowl, beat the egg yolks with the sugar until the mixture becomes thick and creamy. Mix in the butter, melted chocolate, sour cream, and brandy and blend until smooth. Chill for 5 hours. Remove from refrigerator and shape into balls. Roll in cocoa powder. Chill for at least 12 hours before serving.

MAKES 2 POUNDS.

Chapter 19
Romantic Tête-à-Tête

Intimacy is the order of the day when this menu's rustic, primal flavors set the tone. Earthy yet elegant, this meal leaves no other after-dinner choice but romance. Cozy up to a shared plate of Duck Liver Pâté and its rich, red Cabernet Jelly, the latter a simple gourmet shop purchase that makes a world of difference. Then anticipate making eyes at each other over your bowls of Bouillabaisse, a French shellfish soup with seductive aromatics including saffron and fennel. Finally, give yourselves an energizing shot in the arm for dessert. Kahlua Espresso Cake is an invigorating treat that still manages to be smooth, rich, and sinful. It will awaken your senses and send you soaring into post-prandial delight.

THE SONG: *Lady* by Kenny Rogers
THE BEVERAGE: A German Gewurtzraminer

Duck Liver Pâté with Cabernet Jelly

PÂTÉ IS ONE OF THOSE HEADY, ELEMENTAL TREATS, SCINTILLATING FOR ITS INTENSITY OF FLAVOR. IT SOMEHOW MANAGES TO BE AT ONCE RUSTIC AND SPARSE, ELEGANT AND EXOTIC. DUCK AND GOOSE LIVER PÂTÉS ARE THE MOST EXCEPTIONAL. THIS SMOOTH SLAB GETS DRESSED UP EVEN FURTHER WITH A DEEP GARNET CABERNET JELLY PURCHASED AT YOUR LOCAL SPECIALTY FOODS GROCER OR GOURMET SHOP. INTENSELY SATISFYING, THIS IS AN APPETIZER THAT WILL HAVE YOU LANGUIDLY COZYING UP TO EACH OTHER IN NO TIME. SERVE IT WITH A GOBLET OF DEEP RED WINE FOR AN ADDED FLUSH.

8 ounces Riesling white wine
½ pound fresh duck liver, cleaned
½ pound unsalted butter, at room temperature
1 ounce brandy
1 ounce port
Sea salt and freshly ground white pepper to taste
Brioche or toast points for serving

In a saucepan set over high heat, bring the wine to a boil. Add the duck liver, lower the heat to medium high, and simmer for 8 minutes. Remove the liver from the wine and let cool. Combine the liver with the butter, brandy, port, salt, and pepper in a food processor. Blend for 2 minutes or until the mixture reaches a smooth mousse-like consistency. Transfer the mixture to a pâté crock or serving dish with sides. Refrigerate overnight. Serve with toasted brioche or toast points.

MAKES 6 SERVINGS.

Bouillabaisse

THIS IS A BOWL OF APHRODISIACS ONLY THE FRENCH COULD CREATE! CHOCK FULL OF DELEC-TABLE SHELLFISH PERFUMED BY LUXURIOUS SAFFRON, IT WILL INSPIRE YOU AND YOUR MAN TO LOVE WITH HELPLESS ABANDON ONCE YOU'VE SPOONED UP THE LAST DROP. THE FRESH FENNEL AND PARSLEY JOIN THE SHELLFISH AND SAFFRON AS INGREDIENTS SURE TO INDUCE ROMANCE—THEY'VE BEEN REVERED FOR THEIR INVIGORATING PROPERTIES SINCE THE MIDDLE AGES!

¼ cup extra-virgin olive oil
1 celery stick, chopped
½ medium onion, chopped
1 small garlic clove, minced
½ leek, cleaned well and diced
¼ teaspoon fresh thyme
½ bay leaf
1 cup crushed tomatoes
½ cup clam juice
½ cup Sauvignon Blanc (white wine)
⅛ cup fresh fennel, chopped fine
Pinch of saffron
Sea salt and freshly ground white pepper to taste
1 tablespoon fresh parsley, chopped
6 mussels, scrubbed, with beards removed
6 large raw shrimp, peeled and deveined
6 raw sea scallops
1 1-pound lobster, cleaned, rinsed well, and cut into pieces, leaving shell on
½ pound cod, cut into 1-inch cubes

Heat the olive oil in a large soup pot. Add the celery, onion, garlic, leek, thyme, and bay leaf, and cook over medium heat until the onion becomes translucent, about 6 minutes. Add the tomatoes, clam juice, wine, fennel, saffron, salt, and pepper, and simmer for 10 minutes. Toss in the parsley and cook for 5 more minutes. Add the mussels, shrimp, scallops, and lobster, and cook over medium heat for 15 additional minutes. Serve in large soup plates with crusty French bread.

MAKES 2 SERVINGS.

Kahlua Espresso Cake

LIQUEUR, CHOCOLATE, AND DEEP, DARK ESPRESSO COMBINE TO ENLIVEN THIS AFTER-DINNER LAUNCH INTO THE REALM OF ROMANCE. THIS IS A BOLD, GUTSY, REACH-OUT-AND-GRAB-YA DESSERT, ONE THAT SHOWS YOU'RE NOT AFRAID TO MAKE THE FIRST MOVE!

1½ pounds semisweet chocolate, cut into small chunks
1 pound sweet butter
1 cup sugar
¾ cup espresso
1 ounce Kahlua
6 eggs
6 egg yolks

Preheat the oven to 325 degrees F. In the top of a double boiler, melt the chocolate. Add the butter, stir to combine, and remove from heat. In a separate saucepan, heat the coffee and Kahlua until warm and add 1/3 cup sugar, stirring constantly until dissolved. Whisk the coffee mixture into the chocolate mixture, stirring until smooth, and allow the sauce to cool to just above room temperature. Meanwhile, in a separate mixing bowl, whip together the eggs, egg yolks, and remaining sugar until light and foamy. Fold into the cooled chocolate mixture and blend well. Pour the batter into a buttered 10-inch spring-form pan and bake for 45 to 50 minutes. Once cooled, refrigerate the cake for at least 2 hours or preferably overnight. To serve, slice while cold, using a warm knife, and serve at room temperature.

MAKES 6-8 SERVINGS.

Chapter 20
The Second Date

A calculated study in equilibrium, this menu doesn't shy away or come on too strong. It levels the playing field, but still leaves you with the home advantage. Transport yourselves to the easy-going Greek Isles with a first course of lemony shrimp tossed with tangy feta cheese and ripe red tomatoes. Then for balance travel back to the comfort of home with a main dish of American beef. Tenderloin is ideal second-date food. It says quality, but isn't overly assertive or over the top. Plus, this tenderloin's Cognac-kissed red wine marinade really sets it apart. The same can be said for Grilled Asparagus with Béarnaise Sauce. Asparagus woos the palate with its understated elegance. Paired with a zingy, creamy, homemade Béarnaise, it stands out as something special but won't be perceived as too fussy or frivolous. Dessert, spiked as it is with aromatic brandy, will warm your man to the bone and make him linger. Consider it a smooth, caramel embrace—the perfect way to say good-night and rest assured that your second date certainly won't be your last!

THE SONG: *Layla* by Eric Clapton (*Unplugged*)

THE BEVERAGE: Frog's Leap California Cabernet Sauvignon

Greek Shrimp, Feta, and Tomato Salad

THE GREEKS HAVE BEEN ROMANCING FOR CENTURIES, GATHERING STEAM FROM THE FRUITS OF THEIR SUN-DRENCHED ISLES. THIS SALAD FEATURES PLENTY OF TANTALIZING MEDITERRANEAN TREATS—SHRIMP AND OLIVES, TANGY FETA, AND POWERFUL OREGANO. IT'S A DELICIOUSLY LIGHT INTRODUCTION TO YOUR KITCHEN TALENTS—FRESH, FLIRTATIOUS, AND EXOTIC ENOUGH TO KEEP HIS INTEREST PIQUED.

6 tablespoons olive oil
1½ pounds small shrimp, deveined and shelled
3 tablespoons fresh squeezed lemon juice
1 teaspoon white wine vinegar
¼ teaspoon freshly grated lemon zest
1 teaspoon dried oregano, crumbled
Salt
Freshly ground black pepper
6 ounces Feta cheese, coarsely crumbled
3 tomatoes, seeded and chopped
1 cup celery, sliced thin
1 cup Kalamata olives, cut into slivers

Heat 2 tablespoons of the olive oil over high heat in a large, heavy-bottomed skillet. When the oil is very hot, add the shrimp and sauté for 2 minutes or until firm. Transfer the shrimp to a large bowl and allow to cool. In a small mixing bowl, whisk together the lemon juice, vinegar, lemon zest, and oregano, and season to taste with salt and pepper. Add the remaining 4 tablespoons olive oil gradually, whisking until the dressing has emulsified. Add the cheese, tomatoes, celery and olives to the cooled shrimp and toss with the dressing until well coated. Refrigerate until ready to serve. (The salad may be made 1 day ahead and refrigerated, covered, until serving time.)

MAKES 4 SERVINGS.

Red Wine–Marinated Tenderloin Filets

PUT RUBY RED WINE TO WORK IN YOUR FAVOR BY BATHING ULTRA-TENDER BEEF TENDERLOIN IN THIS SEDUCTIVE MARINADE. COOKING WITH WINE ALWAYS MAKES THE MOOD AT THE TABLE EXTRA SPECIAL. SPOIL HIM ON THE SECOND DATE, BUT DO IT UNWITTINGLY. HE'LL BE BACK FOR MORE.

1 USDA Prime beef tenderloin, approximately 4½ pounds, trimmed of fat
2 garlic cloves, peeled and slivered
Salt
Freshly ground black pepper
Red wine marinade (recipe follows)

With the tip of a sharp knife, cut small slits around the entire tenderloin and insert the slivers of garlic. Season the meat generously with salt and pepper, and set it in a shallow roasting pan just large enough to hold the meat tightly. Prepare the marinade and pour it over the meat. Refrigerate overnight. Remove from refrigerator the day of serving and allow to warm to room temperature. Preheat the oven to 425 degrees F. Remove the meat from the marinade and place it in a clean roasting pan. Roast for 10 minutes. Reduce oven heat to 350 degrees F and roast an additional 25 minutes for rare meat (a meat thermometer reading of 120 degrees F), or another 35 minutes for medium (a meat thermometer reading of 130 degrees F). Remove from oven and let stand for 5 to 10 minutes before carving into individually portioned filets.

Red Wine Marinade

¾ cup red wine
¼ cup cognac
¼ cup olive oil
¼ teaspoon dried basil
¼ teaspoon dried parsley
3 tablespoons Worcestershire sauce
2 garlic cloves, crushed
1 teaspoon soy sauce
Freshly ground black pepper to taste

Combine ingredients in a small mixing bowl and stir well. Pour over beef tenderloin (also works nicely for pork tenderloin) and marinate for a minimum of 5 hours or overnight.

MAKES 6 SERVINGS.

Grilled Asparagus with Béarnaise Sauce

SUGGESTIVE SPEARS OF GRILLED GREEN ASPARAGUS TEASE THE PALATE APPETIZINGLY, ESPECIALLY WHEN SLATHERED WITH HOMEMADE BÉARNAISE. ASPARAGUS IS FINGER FOOD DISGUISED. PLAN TO EAT YOUR SPEARS OUT OF HAND, SWIRLING THEM DARINGLY IN A CLOAK OF BÉARNAISE AND NIBBLING OFF THEIR ENDS BIT BY BIT.

10–12 jumbo asparagus spears
Extra-virgin olive oil
Béarnaise sauce (recipe follows)

Rinse and drain the asparagus, and snap off each spear's woody ends. Fill a large sauté pan with just enough water to cover the asparagus when placed in a single layer in the pan. Bring the water to a boil; add the asparagus, and simmer for 3 to 4 minutes, or until bright green in color. Immediately remove the asparagus from the hot water and plunge into an ice water bath (a bowl filled to the brim with ice water and ice cubes). Once cool, remove the asparagus from the cold water and dry with paper towels. Brush the spears with olive oil. Heat a grill to medium high, and grill the asparagus 2 to 3 minutes, just until grill marks appear. Remove from the grill and serve with Béarnaise sauce.

MAKES 2 SERVINGS.

Béarnaise Sauce

TARRAGON MAKES THIS CLASSIC FRENCH SAUCE SHINE. ITS SUBTLE ANISE FLAVOR BRIGHTENS GREEN VEGETABLES, BUT THE SAUCE IS ALSO EXCELLENT WITH A PEPPER-CRUSTED STEAK OR OVEN-BROILED FISH FILET. MAKE A DOUBLE BATCH FOR DATE NUMBER 3 AND REMEMBER TO KEEP THE HEAT IN CHECK DURING THE SAUCE'S PREPARATION. THIS IS ONE CASE WHERE BEING "TOO HOT" IS A FAULT!

2 tablespoons fresh tarragon, chopped coarse, or 2 teaspoons dried tarragon
1 tablespoon tarragon vinegar
$^1/_2$ cup dry white wine
2 shallots, chopped fine
1 teaspoon freshly ground black pepper
3 large egg yolks
$^1/_2$ teaspoon salt
$^3/_4$ cup butter, cut into small chunks

In a small saucepan set over high heat, bring the tarragon, tarragon vinegar, wine, shallots, and pepper to a boil and stir until the liquid is reduced to approximately 2 tablespoons. Set aside. In the top of a double boiler set over medium high heat (water in bottom pan should be simmering, not at a rolling boil), whisk together the egg yolks, 1 tablespoon cold water, and a pinch of salt until thoroughly combined. Strain the reduced wine and add it to the egg yolks. Whisk in the first chunk of butter. When it is completely incorporated, add the next piece. Continue adding the butter, whisking constantly, until all of it has been incorporated and the sauce is thick and fluffy. Serve immediately.

MAKES 2-4 SERVINGS.

Brandied Caramel Flan

GOOD FLAN IS SILKEN, UNCTUOUS, AND JUST FIRM ENOUGH TO CARVE WITH A SPOON. FOLLOW THIS RECIPE TO A T AND YOU'LL BE LAPPING UP CLOUDS OF HEAVENLY CUSTARD. THIS FLAN IS MADE EVEN BETTER BY A DOSE OF WARMING BRANDY, AN IDEAL APRÈS-DINNER DRINK TO POUR ALONGSIDE DESSERT.

3/4 cup sugar plus 1/2 cup more
2 cups milk
2 cups half and half
6 eggs
1/2 teaspoon salt
2 teaspoons vanilla
1/3 cup brandy

Preheat the oven to 325 degrees F. Place 3/4 cup sugar in a large, heavy-bottomed skillet set over medium heat. Stir constantly until the sugar melts and forms a light brown syrup. Immediately transfer the syrup into a warmed shallow glass baking dish or flan pan. Quickly rotate the dish to coat the bottom and sides entirely with the sugar syrup and set aside. To make the custard, heat the milk and half and half in a saucepan until bubbles begin to form around the periphery of the pan. In a mixing bowl, beat the eggs slightly and add the 1/2 cup sugar, salt, and vanilla. Gradually stir in the warm milk mixture and the brandy and blend well. Pour into the prepared baking dish and set the dish in a shallow, ovenproof pan. Boil water in a teakettle or saucepan and pour the boiling water into the pan containing the baking dish, careful to fill with water only halfway up the side of the flan pan. Bake for 35 to 40 minutes, or until a knife inserted into the middle comes out clean. Let cool and then refrigerate for at least 4 hours or overnight. To serve, run a small spatula around the edge of the flan dish and shake gently to release. Invert onto a serving platter.

MAKES 6-8 SERVINGS.

Chapter 21
Snuggled Up Fireside

A knot of arms and legs peeks out from under the flannel wrap. One hand breaks free to cop a bite-sized morsel and warming swill. Seconds later, another hand emerges. Then it's back under wraps again. Fireside dining doesn't get any better than this— warm, cozy, and made to share. This menu is all over the map in terms of flavors, as wandering as those hands under the flannel! Irish Coffee will get things off to a rollicking start, heating you up to a pleasant slow burn as you pop toasty spinach balls into your mouths for sustenance. Then there's the pizza. No cooling slab in a cardboard box awaits you. This pie is fresh and lively, and as tasty at room temperature as it is piping hot. And when dessert rolls around, they'll be no need to tear yourselves away from the fire (or each other). Put out a plate of nutty English toffee, and whisper sweet nothings while you nibble.

THE SONG: *Hot in Herre* by Nelly

THE BEVERAGE: Classic Irish Coffee

Classic Irish Coffee

2 cups hot black coffee
3 ounces Irish whiskey
Sugar
Canned whipped cream
Crème de menthe, preferably green version

Rim 2 stemmed coffee glasses with sugar. Fill each with hot coffee. Divide the Irish whiskey between the glasses and stir to blend. Swirl whipped cream to cover the surface of each glass generously, and drizzle a little crème de menthe on top. Serve immediately.

MAKES 2 SERVINGS.

Toasty Spinach Balls

THEY SAY MAMA KNOWS BEST, AND THIS IS ONE MOTHER'S TRIED AND TRUE RECIPE FOR SNUGGLE FOOD! EASY-TO-PREPARE AND ABSOLUTELY DIVINE, THESE TOASTY ORBS WILL DISAPPEAR QUICKLY, SO DON'T BE TEMPTED TO REDUCE THE RECIPE EVEN THOUGH THERE ARE ONLY THE TWO OF YOU.

6 whole eggs
2 boxes frozen chopped spinach, thawed and well drained (You should
    squeeze all the water out of the spinach with your hands.)
2 cups Pepperidge Farm herb bread stuffing
2 medium onions, chopped fine
1/2 cup celery, chopped fine
3/4 cup butter, melted
1/2 cup Parmesan cheese
1 tablespoon garlic salt
1 1/2 teaspoons dried thyme
1 1/2 teaspoons ground black pepper
1–2 dashes Tabasco sauce

Preheat the oven to 350 degrees F. Beat the eggs in a mixing bowl and set aside. In a separate bowl, mix the spinach, stuffing, onions, celery, melted butter, Parmesan, garlic salt, thyme, pepper, and Tabasco. Add the eggs and blend well until mixture forms a thick paste. Shape into 1-inch balls and bake on a very lightly greased or non-stick cookie sheet for 30 minutes. Serve warm.

MAKES 60-70 BALLS

Fresh Tomato Pizza with Pesto and Goat Cheese

PIZZA MAKES THE PERFECT FIRESIDE DINNER. YOU CAN GRAB A BITE DURING CUDDLE BREAKS AND GET BACK TO THE PLATE WHENEVER YOU'RE ABLE. THIS IS A LIGHT, LIVELY PIZZA, TOPPED WITH FRESH TOMATO ROUNDS AND PUNCHY PESTO. THE GOAT CHEESE PROVIDES ADDED ZIP. FOR HOMEMADE DOUGH, REFER TO THE RECIPE ON PAGE 56 (THE MENU FOR MR. ALL-NIGHTER). IT WILL ELEVATE YOUR PIZZA TO THE EXCEPTIONAL.

4 6-ounce balls pizza dough (see recipe on page 56)
1 cup prepared pesto sauce
1 pound Roma tomatoes, cut into ¼-inch-thick slices
½ pound fresh goat cheese
6 ounces mozzarella, shredded

Preheat the oven to 550 degrees F and preheat your pizza brick or tiles. Place a ball of the dough on a work surface sprinkled with flour or semolina wheat. Using the heels of your hands, press down and flatten the dough. Lift and gently pull the dough into a 6-inch circle. With your fingertips, press a rim around the pizza for a crust. Repeat with the three remaining balls of dough. Spread 1/4 cup of pesto on each pizza round, avoiding the crust. Cover with tomato slices and dollops of goat cheese. Cover each pizza with mozzarella. Bake on the preheated pizza surface for 10 minutes or until the dough has browned and is crisp and the cheese is golden and bubbling.

MAKES 2 SERVINGS.

Peanut-Crusted English Toffee

NO NEED TO GET UP AND GO TO THE DINING ROOM FOR THIS DESSERT. IT'S A NO-MESS SWEET THAT DOESN'T SCRIMP ON RICHNESS. AS DECADENT AS A DENSE SLICE OF CAKE OR PIE, THIS TOFFEE IS POSITIVELY ADDICTIVE. IT'S HARD TO PULL AWAY FROM A PLATE OF IT, SO ONLY PUT OUT A FEW PIECES FOR EACH OF YOU. EITHER THAT, OR PLAN ON A PAUSE IN YOUR SNUGGLES AND A FREE SECOND TO STOKE THE FIRE.

1 cup sugar
1 cup unsalted butter
¼ cup water
1 teaspoon salt
1 teaspoon vanilla
8 ounces semisweet baking chocolate
½ cup peanuts, chopped fine

Spray a 10 x 15-inch baking sheet with cooking spray. In a heavy saucepan, combine the sugar, butter, water, and salt. Bring to a boil over medium-high heat, stirring constantly to dissolve the sugar. Continue boiling, stirring with a wooden spoon, until the toffee is a light caramel color. Remove from heat; stir in the vanilla and salt, and blend well. Immediately pour the toffee onto the baking sheet in a 10 x 10-inch square, using a wooden spoon to shape the toffee. Let stand until completely cooled and hardened or refrigerate until hard. In a double boiler set over low heat, melt 4 ounces of the chocolate. Spread the chocolate over the hardened toffee and sprinkle with 1/4 cup peanuts. Press the nuts into the chocolate lightly, using a sheet of wax paper to cover. Refrigerate for 30 minutes, then melt the remaining chocolate and coat the other side of the toffee with it and press in the remaining 1/4 cup peanuts. Refrigerate an additional 30 minutes. Break the toffee into pieces and store in an airtight container in a cool, dry place.

MAKES 1 POUND.

Chapter 22
Treading Lite-ly

As light as a butterfly on the wind, yet consistent enough to sate, this menu is perfect when the aim is to keep it cool and casual, no strings attached. Congeniality is the message he'll get from a bright glass of homemade Lemon Cocktail, especially when paired with a tray of unsuspecting crudités and Low-Fat Blue Cheese Dip—simple hospitality with a smile. And he won't read any ulterior motives into a tapenade made different by its blend of tuna and bright watercress. He'll make a mental note of your preparedness and unabashed graciousness, of course, but he won't ever dream you whipped up the dish just for him. Same goes for the Summer Salad, a crisp, refreshing blend of cucumbers, tomatoes, red onion, and vitamin-packed parsley. The Cioppino, an Italian fish soup riddled with tomatoes, might make him wonder, given its special-occasion feel. But a little mystery is never a bad thing.

THE SONG: *Nobody Does It Better* by Carly Simon

THE BEVERAGE: Lemon Cocktail

Homemade Lemon Cocktail

LIGHT, BRIGHT, AND AMPLY SPIKED WITH VODKA, THIS IS PORCH SITTIN' SIPPIN' FOR GROWNUPS—
OLD-FASHIONED HOSPITALITY THAT IS AS STRAIGHTFORWARD AND UNSUSPECTING AS IT COMES!

8 ounces Minute Maid Lemonade, preferably with pulp
4 ounces Absolut vodka
2 tall glasses filled with crushed ice and rimmed with sugar
Fresh mint sprigs for garnish

Pour 2 ounces of vodka in each glass. Fill with lemonade. Garnish with a sprig of mint and serve with a striped straw.

MAKES 2 SERVINGS.

Crudités with Low-Fat Blue Cheese Dip

CRUDITÉS, OR FRESH RAW VEGETABLES, SCREAM "CASUAL," OFFERING THE IDEAL MEAL OPENER FOR A MAN WHO DOESN'T WANT TO FEEL CORNERED. PUT OUT CARROTS AND MATCHSTICK SLICES OF CELERY, ADD A RAINBOW OF JULIENNED BELL PEPPER, AND CONSIDER PURCHASING A BELGIAN ENDIVE AND SEPARATING THE LEAVES OUT ON YOUR TRAY FOR PETAL-STYLE DIPPING. THIS BLUE CHEESE DIP TASTES DIVINE WITH ANYTHING RAW AND CRUNCHY AND MAKES THE OLD MAXIM "EAT YOUR VEGETABLES" A NO-BRAINER.

Assorted raw vegetables of your choosing (see head note for recommendations)
1 12-ounce container of fat-free cottage cheese
4 ounces Blue cheese, crumbled

Arrange the vegetables on a platter. Mix the cottage and blue cheese together in a food processor until smooth. Transfer to an attractive bowl for serving, and refrigerate until cool.

MAKES 2 SERVINGS.

Tuna and Watercress Tapenade

TYPICALLY MADE FROM OLIVES, TAPENADE IS A MEDITERRANEAN APPETIZER ENJOYED OVER CASUAL CONVERSATION AT SEASIDE CAFÉS. THIS ORIGINAL TAKE ON THE SPREAD SHOWCASES FRESH WATERCRESS, A FAVORITE GREEN OF THE "LADIES WHO LUNCH" CROWD, PAIRED WITH CANNED TUNA BRIGHTENED BY CAPERS AND FRESH LEMON JUICE. IT SAYS RELAXATION AND RESPITE WITHOUT COMING ON TOO STRONG.

7 ounces canned white tuna in oil, well drained
1/2 cup mayonnaise, preferably Hellmann's
4 ounces cream cheese, at room temperature
2 tablespoons fresh lemon juice
1/4 teaspoon freshly ground black pepper
2 cups watercress, leaves only (approximately 2 bunches)
3 tablespoons capers, drained, rinsed, and dried
4 green onions, white and green parts, chopped

In a food processor, blend the tuna, mayonnaise, cream cheese, lemon juice, and pepper until smooth. Add the watercress leaves, capers, and green onions and pulse periodically until well incorporated but still somewhat chunky. Transfer to an attractive serving bowl and refrigerate 2 hours before serving. Serve with crusty bread, lavash, or crisp crackers of your choosing.

MAKES 4 SERVINGS.

Summer Salad

A WARM WEATHER PALETTE OF REDS AND GREENS, THIS SALAD SPREADS SUNSHINE AND GOOD CHEER. THE PARSLEY LEAVES STAND IN FOR ORDINARY LETTUCE, PROVIDING A VITAMIN-PACKED LIFT TO ENLIVEN YOUR MAN. YOU MAY BE TREADING LIGHTLY, BUT YOU DEFINITELY WANT HIS SPIRITS TO SOAR IN YOUR PRESENCE.

2 medium cucumbers, peeled, seeded, and chopped
2 large tomatoes, seeded and chopped
1 small red onion, chopped fine
1/2 bunch flat leaf parsley, leaves only, minced
1 green bell pepper, seeded and chopped
1/4 cup red wine vinegar
1/2 cup canola oil
Salt
Freshly ground black pepper

Layer cucumbers, tomatoes, red onion, parsley, and bell pepper in an attractive glass serving bowl. In a separate small mixing bowl, whisk together the vinegar and oil and season to taste with salt and pepper. Pour the vinaigrette over the vegetables and toss to coat. Chill before serving.

MAKES 4 SERVINGS.

Cioppino

AN ITALIAN SPECIALTY, CIOPPINO CAPTURES THE LATIN *JOIE DE VIVRE* IN A BOWL. IT'S A FULL-FLAVORED SOUP THAT MANAGES TO FEEL LIGHT AND FESTIVE, THANKS TO THE ADDITION OF CRAB CLAWS AND CLAMS OR MUSSELS. BEACH FOOD AT ITS FINEST, THIS SOUP SETS AN EASY-GOING, CAREFREE MOOD, YET NEVER FAILS TO MAKE A LASTING IMPRESSION.

1 28-ounce can whole tomatoes, liquid reserved, cut into bite-sized chunks
1 16-ounce can stewed tomatoes
1 8-ounce can tomato sauce
1 teaspoon salt
$\frac{1}{2}$ teaspoon pepper
2 teaspoons basil
1 cup white wine
1 dozen cherrystone clams or mussels, cleaned
1 pound fresh whitefish such as halibut or cod
$\frac{1}{3}$ cup olive oil
1 medium onion, chopped
1 cup fresh parsley, chopped
6 cloves garlic
1 pound medium shrimp, peeled and deveined
1 pound crab claws

In a large pot, bring the tomatoes, tomato sauce, salt, pepper, basil, and wine to a boil. Reduce the heat and simmer for 10 minutes. Add the clams or mussels, cover, and cook over medium-low heat for 3 to 5 minutes or until the shells open. Cut the whitefish into 1$\frac{1}{2}$-inch squares and add it to the pot. Remove the pot from heat. In a separate, smaller saucepan, combine the olive oil, onion, parsley, and garlic and bring to a simmer. Add the shrimp and cook for 3 minutes or until the shrimp are just firm. Add the crab claws to the tomato mixture and simmer for 5 more minutes. Transfer the shrimp to the soup and serve warm, not piping hot.

MAKES 6-8 SERVINGS.

White Chocolate Brownies with Dark Chocolate Chips

WHITE IS LIGHT AND BREEZY, AND THESE BROWNIES KEEP THINGS ON EASY STREET WITHOUT ENDING YOUR MEAL ON AN INTENSELY RICH NOTE. DOTTED PLAYFULLY WITH A FEW DARK CHOCOLATE CHIPS, THEY SUGGEST SOMETHING SLIGHTLY DEEPER MIGHT WORK FOR YOU, BUT THEY DEFINITELY DON'T COME ON TOO STRONG!

7 ounces butter
8 ounces white chocolate, grated
2 eggs
$1/4$ teaspoon salt
$1\frac{1}{2}$ teaspoons vanilla
$1\frac{1}{2}$ cups sugar
1 cup flour
1 cup chocolate chips

Preheat the oven to 350 degrees F. Melt the butter over low heat and add half of the grated white chocolate. Do not stir the mixture. In a small mixing bowl, beat the eggs, salt, and vanilla and gradually add the sugar. Add the white chocolate mixture, stir in gently, and add the flour. Fold in the remaining white chocolate and then add the chocolate chips. Bake for 35 minutes in a shallow roasting pan or cookie sheet. Let stand for at least 4 hours before cutting and serving.

MAKES 8 SERVINGS.

SETTING THE STAGE ✦✦✦

GETTING THE MOOD RIGHT FOR THE MOMENT

APHRODISIACS 101

Keep the conversation about the food titillating, and you'll end up having the dessert you are hoping for!

- Dim the lights and fill the room with candles. Wave a Ylang Ylang incense stick around ten minutes before he arrives, and scatter rose petals on the table.

- Make sure your lingerie is on the money! How about a garter or jeweled thong?

- Talk aphrodisiacs! Ask your man if he needs a fork for the oysters or if he prefers to slurp them directly from the shell. Tell him you used some really sweet honey in the lobster sauce and then look him straight in the eyes and ask him if he has a honey he prefers. Explain that you bought female lobsters—that they are the most succulent. Ask him where he'd like to enjoy dessert, etc . . . etc . . .

SETTING THE STAGE ✳✳✳

CAPTURE THAT COMMITMENT

Remember that men always have a strategy for getting their women. You should be no different. This is the time to aim for perfection. Make him think you could get this dinner on the table for his business associates at the drop of a hat – be a natural in the "ways of women." It'll have lasting power.

- Dress in your simply perfect little black dress and add a strand of pearls. Light, fresh, dewy makeup is a key to your charm. Look like the perfect lady.

- Pull out your best china and silverware, and make the table as pretty and perfect as you are.

- Consider setting the table the day before your dinner. That way you can survey the look over time, adding your best porcelain or crystal trinkets (such as Baccarat animals) to the table in an artfully elegant manner.

- Hire a maid service the day before your dinner to make your house look like it's always well kept. Old fashioned wisdom works in your favor here. Make your home the kind of place he will never want to leave!

SETTING THE STAGE ✦

LET'S CELEBRATE

Think fireworks! In fact, purchase some sparklers for some dinnertime fun together. Do what you can to make your date scream fun! This is the time to have chilled champagne on hand and flowing freely.

- Make sure your music is upbeat and soothingly vibrant. No cheesy ballads for this gala evening.

- Infuse your space with bright colors and purchase some solid-color confetti to match your tablecloth. It'll look festive but not gaudy.

- Forgo votives and set a mass of pillar candles in varied sizes on the table.

- Make sure dinner isn't served until after dark. Set the sparklers out by the silverware and go outside. Write sweet nothings in the air to each other just like when you were kids. Try "You are so *hot*," and see where it gets you!

SETTING THE STAGE

THE DEAR JOHN DINNER

Make the whole evening say "Pack your bags!" and "Hit the road, Jack!" He'll get the message. There is little left to say, just carry on with the assurance that you are in control of your destiny.

- Make sure the soup is really cold. Most men don't "get" cold soup. Chances are he'll comment, "My soup is cold." All you have to say is, "I know. I made it special, just for you. Mine is fine." Puzzle him . . . he'll begin to squirm.

- Make sure to set his side of the table with a chair that does not fit properly. Think too high, or better yet, too low! When he complains, say "I'm sorry," and nothing more. If possible, set his chair against a table leg for further discomfort.

- Use your everyday dishes, the most time-worn ones you've got, and paper napkins.

- After dinner, start doing the dishes immediately. Don't accept his help. Tell him you have a busy day tomorrow, and good night. No warm fuzzies here, my dear!

SETTING THE STAGE ✦✳✦

PURE SEDUCTION

If food and passion were ever your secret tools of seduction, now is the time to pull out all the stops! This menu itself is a powerful aphrodisiac, but you should do all you can to set the stage for pure seduction. Sexy is the key word tonight.

- Wear a plunging neckline and a long strand of velvety pearls.

- Dim all the lights and place votives in red glass hurricane lamps or purchase a red lightbulb or two for strategic placement in your living room.

- Use the food to your advantage. Suggest he roll a bead or two of caviar around in his mouth and have him describe the feeling as he gently pops them.

- Make sure your table is intimately set. If you have a large dining table, consider shuffling furniture around and set a small bedside table or outdoor bistro table instead. Or, consider hosting your dinner in the kitchen if you have a sizeable island. Clear the countertops and cover them with candles. A single red rose is all you need in the way of flowers.

- Table linens shouldn't be too fussy for this evening, as you may end up finding alternate uses for the table! Why not set your plates atop a solid-color charger or a neutral placemat? Weave ivy around in between your settings, and spritz the room with a seductive aromatherapy scent an hour before he arrives.

SETTING THE STAGE ✴✦✴

ROMANTIC TÊTE À TÊTE	With this evening, you're headed straight into his arms. Duck liver pâté is as succulent as sweet butter, and grapes have been players in the game of romance for ages–they worked for Cleopatra! Keep the evening intimate and glowing. Everything feels more romantic when the lights are soothing and flattering.

- Enjoy the appetizer together in your clean, candle-lit kitchen with glasses of wine. And tell him he's joining you in the kitchen tonight. He can add the grapes to the fish—just keep an eye on him.

- Offer him nibbles of cheese and olives as you cook, and keep those glasses filled and fresh.

- Flit around the kitchen comfortably, and wear a half-apron that says stylish, not frumpy.

- Make sure you've dabbed a dot of floral perfume on your pulse points, but don't overdo it. As you slip by him, he'll notice.

SETTING THE STAGE ✴✴✴

THE SECOND DATE

You're still in the hook-him mode, and with this easily prepared dinner, you can't go wrong. Almost all the food will be ready before he arrives, so concentrate on looking your best.

- Sexy heels are a must tonight, along with glamorous eyes. Make your gaze haunt him long after he's returned home.

- Let your man light the grill to finish the asparagus. Men love to light grills and he'll delight in your little nod to "needing" him.

- Don't go overboard on the table setting. Keep it contemporary and crisp with two new placemats and a couple of plain white plates. Use interesting napkin rings and original flowers—not roses or tulips—to distinguish your table from others. Pique his curiosity.

- Forgo candlelight until dinnertime, but don't dim the lights too much. Make the candle or candles seem like a festive after-thought—a last-minute touch because things are going well.

- Remember: Asparagus is your secret weapon. Use the spears to your advantage by making them finger food.

SETTING THE STAGE ✳

SNUGGLED UP FIRESIDE

This is an evening all about nibbling and snuggling, so wear something you can romp in and get that fire roaring before he arrives.

- Make sure you've stashed plenty of wood inside, and casually toss a warm, fuzzy throw over the couch for comfort.

- Keep the music low and loving. This might be the time for your favorite old crooners to set the stage for snuggling.

- Forgo flowers and scented candles and burn a bit of spicy incense an hour before he arrives. You want the mood to be cozy and woodsy, even if you're in the middle of the city.

- Make a special trip to Victoria's Secret for some sexy loungewear. You know those outfits you see and wonder if you could wear them in public? Buy one of those!

- Have the makings for a double dose of Irish Coffee on hand, and be generous with your whiskey the second time around.

- Let him handle the fireplace tools—he'll feel the power of the flames.

SETTING THE STAGE ✳✳

TREADING LITE-LY

This meal was created for a relationship that's been established a while. Feeling too full can blow your fun night, so remember to keep the mood as light as the food.

- Freshen up on some cute blonde jokes even if you are a blonde, and don't forget the punchlines!

- Eat the appetizers in style outdoors, weather permitting, but bring your date inside for the Cioppino.

- Set your indoor table casually. Think summer sun and simple, languid days, and make your linens match the mood.

- Place a bowl between you for discarding shells, and make up some little finger bowls afloat with fresh lemon for post-soup clean-up.

- After dinner, leave everything on the table and suggest a stroll outdoors. Wandering a park or the neighborhood hand-in-hand should send him straight back to your home for a "nightcap."

CUNNING CONCOCTIONS

A GUIDE TO ENTICING ELIXIRS AND NIBBLES TO SUIT THE MOOD

THE MOOD AND THE SONG	TO SIP	TO NIBBLE
APHRODISIACS 101	**FROZEN MINT DAIQUIRI**	**TARAMASALATA**
Come Away with Me by Norah Jones	4 ounces light rum 2 tablespoons fresh lime juice 16 mint leaves 2 teaspoons sugar *Combine all ingredients with a cup of ice and blend at high speed. Pour into glasses, Garnish with mint sprig and lime wheel.*	½ loaf stale white bread, crusts removed 1 medium onion 1 garlic clove 2 to 3 cups olive oil 1 tablespoon dried parsley 1 teaspoon cumin 1 teaspoon dried oregano 1 jar tarama (fish roe) Juice of 1 lemon *Soak bread in water to cover until soggy. Squeeze out water as you would a sponge. Chop onion and garlic in a food processor. Add herbs. Add fish roe and bread. Add 1 cup oil and puree until smooth. With machine running, add more oil until very smooth. Add lemon juice. Refrigerate and serve.*
CAPTURE THAT COMMITMENT	**CANAL STREET DAISY**	**HERB SPINACH BALLS**
White Flag by Dido	Juice of ½ lemon Juice of ½ orange 2 ounces Dewar's whiskey Soda water *Mix lemon and orange juices and whisky and pour into tall glass with ice. Top with soda.*	See recipe p.128.

CUNNING CONCOCTIONS

THE MOOD AND THE SONG	TO SIP	TO NIBBLE
LET'S CELEBRATE	**BELLINI**	**PECAN CHEESE WAFERS**
Walking on Sunshine by Katrina and the Waves	4 ounces peach nectar or pureed peach pulp 4 ounces champagne Dash of lemon juice Dash of grenadine *Divide chilled peach nectar between two champagne flutes. Add dash of lemon, top with champagne and grenadine. Serve chilled.*	½ cup softened butter 8 ounces grated Cheddar 1 cup flour 1 teaspoon salt ½ teaspoon black pepper ¼ teaspoon cayenne pepper 1 cup coarsely chopped pecans *Beat butter and cheese together until smooth. Add dry ingredients and combine. Divide in half. Form each half into a log in waxed paper. Chill until firm. Slice into ¼-inch-thick rounds. Bake on a lightly greased sheet at 350 degrees F for 10 to 12 minutes.*
THE DEAR JOHN DINNER	**FARE THEE WELL**	**CREAMY BABY SHRIMP DIP**
I Will Survive by Gloria Gaynor	3 ounces gin 1 ounce dry vermouth 2 ounces sweet vermouth 2 dashes triple sec *Shake all ingredients in an ice-filled cocktail shaker until cold and strain into martini glasses.*	3 3-ounce packages cream cheese 1 stick butter 2 tablespoons mayonnaise 2 tablespoons lemon juice 1 teaspoon Worcestershire 1 cup celery, chopped 1 small onion, chopped Dash of salt and pepper 12 ounces cooked shrimp, cut into ¼-inch pieces. *Mix together cream cheese and butter until smooth. Add lemon juice, mayonnaise, and Worcestershire sauce. Add celery and onion and blend. Add shrimp. Season. Serve.*

CUNNING CONCOCTIONS ✳✳✳

THE MOOD AND THE SONG	TO SIP	TO NIBBLE
THE MORNING AFTER	**PURPLE PASSION**	**TOMATO BRUSCHETTA**
Love Me Two Times by The Doors	4 ounces Absolut vodka 6 ounces grapefruit juice 6 ounces Welch's purple grape juice Sugar to taste *Mix ingredients together and pour over ice to serve.*	1 ripe tomato, diced fine 2 garlic cloves, minced 2 tablespoons extra-virgin olive oil 1 tablespoon balsamic vinegar ½ teaspoon sea salt Freshly ground black pepper 5 fresh basil leaves, julienned Parmesan shavings 1 baguette, sliced into rounds *Place tomato in a bowl. Add garlic, oil, vinegar, salt, and pepper. Mix and let stand at room temperature for 30 minutes. Toast bread lightly and top with tomato mixture. Garnish with basil and Parmesan.*
PURE SEDUCTION	**BANSHEE**	**COEUR A LA CRÈME**
Easy Living by Billie Holiday	2 ounces crème de banana 1 ounce white crème de cacao 1 ounce half & half *Shake ingredients over cracked ice and strain into cocktail glasses.*	1 pound cottage cheese 1 pound soft cream cheese ½ teaspoon salt 2 cups heavy cream ½ cup strawberries, crushed *Combine cottage cheese, cream cheese, and salt. Mix, using a hand mixer set on low speed, gradually adding the cream. Spread into a heart-shaped mold lined with a single layer of cheesecloth and refrigerate overnight inverted on a plate to drain. Remove from mold. Serve topped with strawberries.*

CUNNING CONCOCTIONS ✦✦✦

THE MOOD AND THE SONG	TO SIP	TO NIBBLE
ROMANTIC TÊTE-À-TÊTE	**PINEAPPLE COOLER**	**ARTICHOKES WITH LEMON MAYO**
Do You Believe in Magic by The Lovin' Spoonful	2 ounces pineapple juice ½ teaspoon powdered sugar 2 ounces white wine 2 ounces soda water *Mix together juice, sugar, and wine. Pour over ice. Top with soda water and stir. Garnish with lemon peel spiral.*	2 large artichokes 1 lemon, cut in half *Clean and trim artichokes. Cut tips off leaves. Cover with water, add lemons, and bring water to a boil. Reduce heat and simmer 30 minutes. Remove from water and drain upside down. Whisk fresh lemon juice into store-bought mayo and serve.*
THE SECOND DATE	**MR. MANHATTAN**	**SPICY OLIVES**
You Make Loving Fun by Fleetwood Mac	2 lumps sugar 8 mint sprigs ½ teaspoon lemon juice 2 teaspoons orange juice 3 ounces gin *Muddle sugar and mint. Mix with juices and gin and shake well. Strain into cocktail glasses and serve.*	¼ cup extra-virgin olive oil 2½ tablespoons red wine vinegar 1¼ teaspoons red pepper flakes 4 garlic cloves, minced ½ pound oil-cured black olives ½ pound green olives (with pits) *Combine oil and vinegar and mix well. Pour over olives and toss to coat. Refrigerate for 24 hours or up to 2 weeks.*

CUNNING CONCOCTIONS *

THE MOOD AND THE SONG	TO SIP	TO NIBBLE
SNUGGLED UP FIRESIDE	**PORT WINE COBBLER**	**COGNAC ROQUEFORT SPREAD**
Mr. Man by Alicia Keys with Jimmy Cozier	2 teaspoons powdered sugar 4 ounces soda water 3 ounces port Fresh seasonal berries *Dissolve sugar in soda water and pour into shaved ice–filled wine goblets. Pour in port and stir. Garnish w/berries. Serve with a straw.*	1 pound Roquefort blue cheese 1 stick unsalted butter ¼ teaspoon cayenne pepper ⅓ cup Courvoisier cognac *Blend cheese and butter in the bowl of a food processor. Add the cayenne and cognac. Blend until smooth. Serve with assorted crackers.*
TREADING LITE-LY	**STOLI DOLI**	**ITALIAN TUNA DIP**
Happy Together by The Turtles	1 fresh Dole pineapple, cut into 2-inch chunks Stoli's vodka to submerge pineapple in a glass container, covered *In a glass container, cover pineapple with vodka for 4 days at room temperature. Strain, chill, and serve the juice. Do not eat fruit.*	1 can solid white tuna 1 4-ounce package Zesty Italian salad dressing mix 8 ounces sour cream Parsley for garnish *Break up tuna with a fork in a serving bowl. Add dressing mix and sour cream. Mix well. Garnish with parsley.*

part 3

Dreamboat Dream Menus

This chapter features the dream menus of some of the world's most desirable men—film and TV stars, industrialists, heirs, and even sexy celebrity chefs. Their ultimate meals for sure-fire seduction are collected here for your inspiration. The saying goes, "Imitation is the finest form of flattery," so go ahead and copy these guys; they're used to it. These menus feature many of the men's own recipes—tried and true formulas they've used for snagging their loves. In fact, perfectly executing each dreamboat's meal could make him yours, if only you could figure out a way to get your hands on him!

These stars' works of kitchen art range from the excessively simple Baked Chicken in a Curried Cream Sauce whipped up by Coca-Cola heir and racecar enthusiast John Woodruff, to the sublime Tartine of Squab "en Salmis" expertly prepared by leading New York chef Daniel Boulud. Ted Turner's heart-warming Bison Chili with Cheddar Cheese, Onion, and Jalapeño conjures up Rocky Mountain nights and deep-pocketed out-doorsmen; while TV-actor-cum-chef Mitchell Anderson heats things up with a racy Beet Green Ravioli with Golden Beet Sauce and Red Beet Stick garnish. What's best is that these men haven't stopped with dinner. Each selected man has added a drink and song preference to match his meal, supply-ing further insider information you'll find perfectly irresistible.

Chapter 23
Peter Fonda

This Easy Rider likes his sustenance earthy and organic, punctuated by the smooth, natural sweetness of honey. This is a meal that oozes casual confidence and understated cool, ideal for revving up that fine-tuned engine. Fonda's tastes tend toward the fresh and natural, with the invigorating addition of flavors masculine, rustic, and wild!

THE SONG: *Tupelo Honey* by Van Morrison
THE WINE: A well-chilled Pinot Grigio

Mixed Organic Greens with Balsamic Vinaigrette

A TIMELESS CULT ICON, PETER FONDA KNOWS THAT FOOD FADS CAN FIZZLE AND DIE AS FAST AS ILL-FATED, TREND-CONSCIOUS FILM STARS. HE KEEPS HIS KITCHEN OF THE MOMENT BY HEEDING THE CALL OF THE WILD. NO FUNKY, FUSION-FOOD CONFUSION FOR FONDA. INSTEAD, THIS LOVER OF ALL THINGS NATURAL OPTS FOR A SIMPLE BOWL OF ORGANIC GREENS TOSSED WITH WELL-AGED BALSAMIC VINEGAR. TAKE IT FROM FONDA: THE OLDER THE BALSAMIC, THE SWEETER AND MORE COMPLEX.

1 handful organic baby arugula, cleaned and dried
1 handful organic radicchio leaves, cleaned and dried
1 handful fresh organic spinach, cleaned and dried
1 handful organic endive leaves, cleaned and dried
One handful organic baby romaine, cleaned and dried
⅓ cup aged, high-quality balsamic vinegar
¾ cup imported extra-virgin olive oil
1 teaspoon honey
Sea salt
Pepper
Parmigiano-Reggiano cheese

Place cleaned and well-dried greens in a large bowl and toss to blend. In a separate bowl, measure 1/3 cup balsamic vinegar and gradually add 3/4 cup olive oil in a slow, steady stream, whisking continually until the mixture is thoroughly blended and almost "creamy" in appearance. Add the honey and continue stirring. Add 1/4 teaspoon sea salt and 1/4 teaspoon freshly ground pepper.

Dress greens with about 1/3 of the vinaigrette and toss to coat lightly. Do not saturate the greens in dressing. Transfer the dressed greens to a serving plate and top with slices of fresh Parmigiano-Reggiano cheese. Serve immediately.

MAKES 2 SERVINGS..

Risotto a la Fungi

EARTHY AND *SAUVAGE*, WILD MUSHROOM RISOTTO WILL MAKE ANY MAN OF THE ROAD WILLING TO COME IN AND COZY UP. FONDA LOVES THE BEGUILING FLAVOR THAT WILD MUSHROOMS SUCH AS CHANTERELLES, PORCINIS, AND SHIITAKES IMPART TO RISOTTO. SO MAKE YOUR RATIO OF WILD TO BUTTON MUSHROOMS AT LEAST 2 TO 1 TO DO JUSTICE TO HIS HEARTY, HEADY, AROMATIC DISH.

3 to 4 cups mushroom stock (chicken or vegetable stock can be substituted)
3 teaspoons olive oil
½ of a sweet Vidalia onion, minced
¾ cup short-grain Italian arborio rice
1½ tablespoons unsalted butter at room temperature
2 cups mixed wild (shiitake, oyster, chanterelle, porcini) and white button
  mushrooms
½ cup freshly grated Parmesan cheese, plus more as needed

Sauté the mushrooms in 1 teaspoon olive oil and set aside. In a separate saucepan, bring the stock to a simmer. Meanwhile, heat the remaining 2 teaspoons olive oil in a heavy-bottomed 2-quart saucepan and cook the onion, stirring over medium heat until translucent. Add the rice and stir to coat thoroughly with the oil. Raise the heat to medium-high and add the simmering stock to the rice a ladle at a time. The broth should remain at a simmer. Stir constantly. Once the stock has fully absorbed into the rice mixture, add another ladle of stock and continue stirring until it, too, is fully absorbed. Repeat, stirring constantly, until all the stock has been used. This should take approximately 20 to 30 minutes. If the rice grains are still hard once all the stock has been added, supplement with ladles of boiling water added in the same manner as the stock until the rice reaches the desired doneness. The rice should be creamy and tender on the outside, yet still slightly resist when bitten. Stir in the sautéed mushrooms and remove the pan from heat. Add the butter and cheese and continue stirring. Season to taste with salt and pepper. Serve immediately with additional grated Parmesan to garnish.

MAKES 2 SERVINGS.

White Chocolate Chunk Cheesecake

NOTHING CHEESY ABOUT THIS TIMELESS DESSERT. IT'S AS SUAVE AS THIS MAN AND DELIGHTFULLY UNPREDICTABLE, RIDDLED AS IT IS WITH WHITE CHOCOLATE AND KISSED WITH CINNAMON. THIS IS THE UNEXPECTED AT ITS BEST.

2 cups graham cracker crumbs
½ cup butter, melted
3 pounds cream cheese, at room temperature
2 cups sugar mixed with 1 tablespoon cinnamon
2 teaspoons vanilla
7 eggs
2½ cups white chocolate chunks plus ½ cup for garnish
1 cup whipping cream

Preheat the oven to 300 degrees F. Mix together the graham cracker crumbs and melted butter. Line a 10-inch springform pan with parchment paper, then press the crumb mixture into the bottom of the pan. Bake for 10 minutes, remove from oven, and allow to cool. In a medium mixing bowl, beat the cream cheese, sugar, and cinnamon until smooth. Add the vanilla and eggs, mixing until just incorporated. Do not over mix. Stir in the chocolate and pour the mixture over the cooled crust. Tear a large piece of aluminum foil and place the pan on it. Wrap the foil up around the sides of the pan and up above the cheesecake, forming a tent. Seal the foil firmly at the top. Place the foil-wrapped cheesecake in a larger baking pan and fill with water to reach 3/4 of the way up the side of the springform pan. Bake for 3 hours. Remove the cheesecake from the oven and foil tent and cool at room temperature for at least 2 hours. Chill overnight in the springform pan. Garnish with whipped cream and white chocolate shavings (see Note).

MAKES 6 SERVINGS.

Note: Create white chocolate shavings by "peeling" the chocolate chunk with a sharp vegetable peeler.

Chapter 24
Ted Turner and George McKerrow for Ted's Montana Grill

Media mogul and western land man Ted Turner, in cahoots with business partner George McKerrow of Longhorn Steakhouse fame, has corralled a herd of carnivorous followers. Turner's disciples gather nightly for sustenance at the entrepreneurs' latest venture, Ted's Montana Grill, where America's best selection of Native American bison is served with panache. In the mood for the romance of the Old West? This is a hungry man's meal sure to get your cowboy into the saddle. Turner's menu will transport you to wilder places—a land where you can do-si-do around your man until he kicks off his boots with promises never to hit the trail again.

THE SONG: *You Can't Roller Skate in a Buffalo Herd* by Roger Miller

THE BEVERAGE: Big Sky Lemonade

Big Sky Lemonade

BRIGHT, SPRITE, AND STIFF ENOUGH FOR ANY RUGGED MAN OF THE WEST, THIS LEMONADE TAKES TRADITIONAL HOSPITALITY TO THE NEXT LEVEL. MAKE A PITCHER AND SETTLE IN FOR SOME FUN.

1 ounce Buffalo Trace bourbon
1 ounce Cointreau
2 cups lemonade

Fill a highball glass with ice cubes. Pour bourbon and Cointreau into a cocktail shaker and shake vigorously to blend. Pour over ice and top off with lemonade. Stir.

MAKES 2 SERVINGS.

Bison Chili with Cheddar Cheese, Onion, and Jalapeño

A BOWL OF CHILI MAKES FOR GREAT "WALKIN' FOOD." PILE THIS FEISTY FAVORITE HIGH WITH CHEESE, CHOPPED ONION, AND JALAPEÑO AND ROAM THE RANGE TOGETHER. IF YOU MUST SIT STILL (OR DON'T HAVE MUCH OF A RANGE TO WANDER), PULL UP A PORCH ROCKER OR TWO AND SPOON-FEED YOURSELVES THIS COWBOY CLASSIC MADE BETTER BY THE ADDITION OF NATIVE AMERICA'S FINEST RED MEAT. BISON IS LEAN AND TASTY, AND THANKS TO TURNER AND OTHER WESTERN RANCHERS, IT'S MAKING A GREAT COMEBACK.

2$\frac{1}{2}$ pounds coarsely ground bison (see Note)
1 cup onion, diced
1 tablespoon minced garlic
1 quart warm water
5 ounces beef base
1 cup plus 1 tablespoon tomato paste
1 teaspoon fresh oregano leaves
$\frac{1}{4}$ teaspoon cayenne pepper
$\frac{1}{2}$ teaspoon black pepper
1$\frac{1}{2}$ teaspoon sugar
2$\frac{1}{2}$ teaspoons ground cumin
1$\frac{1}{2}$ ounce chili powder

1 cup canned diced tomatoes
1 cup canned ranch style beans
Shredded cheddar cheese, chopped onions, sliced fresh jalapeños for garnish

Heat a large, heavy-bottomed Dutch oven or saucepan over high heat for 5 minutes. Add the bison and stir to break up the meat into small grounds. When the meat is browned, but not yet cooked through, add the onion and garlic and continue cooking. When the onions are transparent and tender, lower the heat. In a mixing bowl, combine the water, beef base, and tomato paste and whisk until thoroughly combined. Add this mixture to the bison and bring to a boil. Add the oregano, cayenne, pepper, sugar, cumin, and chili powder, and reduce the heat to a simmer. Cook for 15 minutes, then add the tomatoes and beans. Simmer for an additional minute. Remove from heat, top with garnishes, and serve alongside an iceberg wedge.

MAKES 6 SERVINGS.

Note: Bison must be cut and ground from whole chuck roast, never rely on the $^3/_8$-inch ground, packaged bison.

Iceberg Wedge with "BLT" Dressing

A STEAKHOUSE CLASSIC COMES HOME WITH THIS MASCULINE SALAD THAT IS LONG ON FLAVOR. BACON AND RANCH DRESSING PAIR UP TO MAKE OLD-FASHIONED ICEBERG LETTUCE A TREAT. THE DRESSING WILL KEEP FOR SEVERAL DAYS IN YOUR REFRIGERATOR, AND IS A DELICIOUS DIP FOR CRUDITÉS, TOO.

1 head iceberg lettuce, well chilled and quartered
4 cups ranch salad dressing
$^3/_4$ cup chives, chopped into $^1/_8$-inch lengths
$^3/_4$ cup fresh tomatoes, diced
$^3/_4$ cup cooked bacon, crumbled
$1^1/_2$ tablespoons warm bacon grease

Place an iceberg quarter on a plate. In a small mixing bowl, whisk together the ranch dressing, chives, tomatoes, bacon, and bacon grease until well incorporated. Pour over the lettuce wedge and serve.

MAKES 4 SERVINGS.

Strawberry Shortcake

TURNER MAY BE THE WEST'S LARGEST PRIVATE LANDOWNER, BUT HE'S A SOUTHERN BOY TOO. WHAT THIS GEOGRAPHICAL DUALITY MEANS IS THAT THIS DESIRABLE MOGUL PLACES A PREMIUM ON DOWN-HOME HOSPITALITY, WHEREVER HE'S HANGING HIS HAT. STRAWBERRY SHORTCAKE IS A DESSERT THAT SAYS HOME WHEREVER IT'S SERVED. IT'S A GREAT CLOSING TO THIS MEAL, BUT ALSO FABULOUS SERVED ALONE WITH A STIFF BLACK CUP O' JOE WHENEVER YOUR MAN MIGHT WANDER IN.

FOR THE SHORTCAKE:
3 cups pastry flour
4 teaspoons cream of tartar
3½ teaspoons baking soda
½ teaspoon iodized salt
¼ cup granulated sugar
8 ounces well-chilled unsalted butter, cut into ½-inch chunks
1 cup half and half

FOR THE STRAWBERRY SAUCE:
1 pound fresh strawberries, quartered
¼ cup granulated sugar
2 cups frozen strawberries with their juice, thawed

FOR THE TOPPING:
1 cup heavy whipping cream
2 tablespoons granulated sugar
2 teaspoons vanilla extract

FOR ASSEMBLY:
1 quart vanilla ice cream

Place the flour, cream of tartar, baking soda, salt, and sugar in the bowl of a food processor and blend well. Add the butter, pulsing the processor on and off until a coarse meal forms. When the butter bits are no larger than pea-size, transfer the flour mixture to a stand mixer fitted with a paddle attachment and mix over low speed, gradually adding the half and half. When a loose ball has formed, remove the dough from the mixer and transfer it to a stainless steel bowl. Cover with plastic wrap and refrigerate for 30 minutes. Line a baking sheet with parchment paper and pre-heat the oven to 325 degrees F. If you have a convection oven, use the low fan set-ting. When the dough is cold, transfer it bit by bit to a 1/4-cup measuring cup and level off. Invert the dough onto the parchment paper and press the rounds down using your hands, to achieve 12 3-inch discs approximately 1½-inch thick. Bake for 9 minutes, turn the sheet pan, and bake an additional 9 minutes or until golden brown. Remove from oven and allow to cool completely. Meanwhile, place the fresh straw-berries in a bowl and add the sugar, tossing well to coat. Allow to sit for 2 hours for best results. Place the thawed frozen berries with their juice into the bowl of a food processor and puree until smooth. When the fresh strawberries have absorbed their sugar and released their juices, add the frozen puree and blend thoroughly. In a sep-arate mixing bowl, combine the heavy cream, sugar, and vanilla and whip until the cream holds soft peaks. Cut off the top third of a cooled shortcake and place it in a cold, large rimmed serving bowl. Begin the layering of the shortcake by adding 1/3 of the strawberries and 2 scoops of vanilla ice cream to the cake. Continue layering, ending with the whipped cream on the uppermost cake round. Drizzle the cream-topped final layer with a few strawberries and ample juice to garnish.

MAKES 6 SERVINGS.

Chapter 25
Daniel Boulud

What woman doesn't swoon at the thought of a self-assured French chef taking over her kitchen and hand feeding her delectables with a certain je ne sais quoi? Gallic superchef Daniel Boulud has come a long way from the family farm near Lyon. This man seduces Manhattanites and Palm Beach's jet set with his inspired culinary creations nightly. In addition to overseeing five much-heralded restaurants, an exclusive catering business, and a line of kitchenware and Caspian caviar, this French wonder has authored five cookbooks. Boulud appears regularly on television, and works tirelessly for charity as well. Here he shares three of his celebrated recipes for wooing your man.

THE SONG: Sensual Brazilian jazz such as João Gilberto

THE BEVERAGES: Pirorat (Spain) Alvaro Palacios "Les Terrasses" 1998 with the squab; Fattoria Le Pupille "Sol Alto" 2000 from Maremma, Tuscany, Italy, for dessert.

Chestnut, Celery Root, and Apple Soup*

FLAVORS OF FALL COMBINE IN THIS DELICATE SOUP, INVITING YOU TO COZY UP TOGETHER SOFTLY AND WHISPER SWEET NOTHINGS. AT ONCE HOMEY AND SOPHISTICATED, THIS SMOOTH, CREAMY CONCOCTION WILL WORK ITS MAGIC WITH THE FIRST SPOONFUL. SERVE IT VERY HOT IN PRE-HEATED BOWLS.

2 tablespoons extra-virgin olive oil
1 medium onion, peeled, trimmed, and sliced thin
1 medium leek, white part only, trimmed, sliced thin, washed, and dried
2 McIntosh apples, peeled, cored, and cut into 1/2-inch cubes
10 ounces celery root, peeled and cut into 1/2-inch cubes
1 bay leaf
1 sprig thyme
Pinch of freshly grated nutmeg
Salt and freshly ground white pepper
3/4 pound peeled fresh chestnuts from 1 1/4 pounds chestnuts in shells; or 3/4 pound dry-packed bottled or vacuum-sealed peeled chestnuts
2 quarts homemade unsalted chicken stock or store-bought low-sodium chicken broth
1/2 cup heavy cream

Heat the oil in a stockpot or large casserole over medium heat. Add the onion, leek, apples, celery root, bay leaf, thyme, nutmeg, salt, and pepper and cook, stirring occasionally, for about 10 minutes, or until the onions and leeks are soft but not colored. Add the chestnuts and chicken stock and bring to a boil. Lower the heat to a simmer and cook, skimming the surface regularly, 35 to 40 minutes, or until the chestnuts can be mashed easily with a fork. Add the heavy cream and simmer 5 to 10 minutes more, then discard the bay leaf and thyme. Puree the soup until smooth using a blender, food processor, or hand-held immersion blender, then pass it through a fine-mesh strainer. At this point, you should have about 2 quarts of soup. If you have more, or if you think the soup is too thin—the soup should have the consistency of a veloute or light cream soup—simmer it over medium heat until thickened.

* From Daniel Boulud's *Café Boulud Cookbook*. Daniel Boulud and Dorie Greenspan. Scribner, 1999.

Taste, and if necessary, adjust the seasoning. (The soup can be cooled completely and stored in a covered jar in the refrigerator for 3 to 4 days or frozen for up to a month. Bring the soup back to a boil before serving.) To serve: Reheat the soup, if necessary—the soup really needs to be hot—and ladle it into warm bowls.

MAKES 4 SERVINGS.

Tartine of Squab "En Salmis"*

HAUTE CUISINE LENDS A FESTIVE AIR TO THE OCCASION, AND THIS SUAVE TARTINE WILL CERTAINLY IMPRESS. THIS RECIPE INVOLVES SOME CULINARY KNOW-HOW, BUT DON'T LET IT INTIMIDATE YOU. THE RESULTS WILL BE WELL WORTH YOUR EFFORTS. BOULUD SUGGESTS YOU DROP ALL INHIBITIONS AND EAT THIS WITH YOUR HANDS. THIS WILL BE THE MOST SUBLIME OPEN-FACED SANDWICH YOUR MAN HAS EVER HAD.

4 squab (14 to 16 ounces each), head removed, legs, wings, necks, and backbone
   removed and reserved
4 tablespoons unsalted butter
1/4 cup cognac or brandy
2 cups unsalted chicken stock or store-bought low-sodium chicken broth
1 tablespoon sherry vinegar
Salt and freshly ground pepper
1 tablespoon extra-virgin olive oil
1 pound wild mushrooms, trimmed, cleaned, and sliced thin
1 shallot, peeled, trimmed, and sliced thin
4 slices sourdough bread
1 clove garlic, peeled and halved
4 2-ounce portions fresh foie gras

Center a rack in the oven and preheat the oven to 400 degrees F. Chop the back, wings, and neck bones into small pieces. Melt 2 tablespoons of the butter in a large sauté pan over high heat. Add the bones and legs and cook until golden brown. Deglaze and flambé with the cognac and cook until the liquid has evaporated. Add the chicken stock and lower the heat to a simmer; cook until the leg meat is tender, approximately 20 minutes. Remove the legs from the pan and let cool. Season the pan with the sherry vinegar, salt, and pepper and reduce the liquid by half. Strain the sauce through a fine-mesh sieve. Once the legs are cool enough to handle, remove the leg meat from the bones and chop fine. In a large sauté pan over high heat, warm the olive oil. Add the mushrooms and shallots and cook until all the liquid in

* From Chef Daniel Boulud's *Cooking in New York City*. Daniel Boulud and Peter Kaminsky. Assouline, 2002

the pan has evaporated. Once cool, chop the mushroom mixture fine and combine with the braised leg meat. Season with salt and pepper. Season the squab breasts with salt and pepper. In a large ovenproof sauté pan, melt the remaining 2 tablespoons of butter. Sear the breasts, skin side down, until golden brown. Flip the breasts over, place the pan in the oven, and roast for 4 minutes. Remove the pan from the oven and place the squab on a wire rack to rest for a few minutes. Remove the breast meat from the bones and cut the breast into thin slices. Set aside and keep warm. Prepare a very hot grill. Rub the sliced sourdough bread with the cut garlic. Grill the bread on both sides to obtain a good charred flavor. While the bread is grilling, in a large sauté pan over medium-high heat, cook the foie gras for 3 minutes on each side. Drain the foie gras on layers of paper towels. Divide the mushroom leg mixture evenly among the toasted sliced bread. Place a piece of foie gras on top of the mushroom mixture and place the sliced breast meat on top of the foie gras. Keep warm. Warm the sauce, if necessary. Place the assembled bread slices on the center of four warm dinner plates. Spoon the sauce over the squab meat and around the plate.

MAKES 4 SERVINGS.

Pineapple and Coconut Givre*

THIS DELIGHTFUL DESSERT IS ONE CHEF DANIEL IS SURE YOU CAN HANDLE AT HOME. IT WILL TRANSPORT YOU AND YOUR MAN TO A TROPICAL PARADISE, WHERE SUN, SAND, AND RIPE FRUITS MAKE LOVING SECOND NATURE.

FOR THE GIVRE:
1 very ripe pineapple
One 15-ounce can Coco Lopez
1/4 cup dark rum
Freshly squeezed juice of 1/2 lime

FOR THE DECORATION:
2 cups sugar
1/4 cup light corn syrup

* From *Daniel's Dish: Entertaining at Home with a Four Star Chef*. Daniel Boulud, Filipacchi Publishing, 2003

To make the Givre: Trim the base of the pineapple so that it sits flat. Cut off the top 2 inches of the pineapple, leaves still attached. Carefully cut to separate the crown of leaves from the fruit cap; discard the cap, reserving the leaves intact. Using a small knife and a spoon, scoop out the pineapple pulp over a bowl, dropping the fruit and all the juice you can catch into the bowl and taking care not to pierce the shell. Holding the pineapple upside down, scrape the inside to remove any remaining pulp. Rinse the shell under cold running water. Pat dry, wrap in plastic wrap, and freeze for at least 2 hours or overnight. Put the fruit and juice into a food processor; process until smooth. Strain the juice through a fine-mesh sieve (there will be about 4 cups); discard the pulp. Stir together the pineapple juice, Coco Lopez, rum, and lime juice. Refrigerate overnight. Churn the cold pineapple mixture in an ice-cream maker following the manufacturer's instructions. Working quickly, unwrap the frozen pineapple, fill it just to the top with the sorbet, and return it to the freezer along with the unused portion of sorbet.

To make the decorations: Line a work surface and three baking sheets with parchment paper; lightly coat with vegetable spray. Prepare an ice-water bath in a large bowl. Bring the sugar and 1/2 cup water to a boil in a heavy, medium saucepan. Stir until the sugar dissolves, washing down any sugar crystals from the sides of the pan with a wet brush. Bring the syrup to a boil—don't stir—and cook until light golden brown. Remove the pan from heat and immerse the bottom of the pan in the ice water for 30 seconds. Set the pan down on a heatproof surface and let the caramel rest until it forms a thin thread when drizzled, about 8 minutes. Lightly coat the handles of two wooden spoons with vegetable spray. Set four soup cans on the parchment paper-lined surface. Rest one end of each spoon on a separate soup the spoons should be parallel to each other and about 15 inches apart. Intertwine the tines of two forks and hold them one hand. Dip the tines into the warm caramel, letting the excess drip back into the pot. Rapidly wave the tines back and forth over the middle portion of the two spoons to create a series of sugar threads. Repeat a couple of times, until you have a light, airy layer of spun sugar. If the caramel in the pot hardens, warm it over low heat. Gently place the spun sugar layer on a prepared baking sheet. Continue spinning sugar layers until you have enough to form a base for the pineapple givre.

To serve: Place the givre on a large platter. Cover the givre with scoops of the unused sorbet and top with the reserved pineapple crown leaves. Make a spun sugar base for the pineapple—it should be as light and lovely as a golden cloud.

MAKES 10 SERVINGS.

Chapter 26
Mitchell Anderson

This multi-talented man has wooed from the stage and the TV screen, starring in such diverse productions as *Doogie Howser, MD; Party of Five; The Karen Carpenter Story; Relax, It's Just Sex;* and many other film, television, and stage projects, but his heart also has a home in the kitchen. From the age of eight, Anderson has had a love of baking and cooking, an infatuation he has turned into a thriving second career. As a partner in Souper Jenny, a unique Atlanta eatery, Anderson helped to create gourmet soups, salads, and sandwiches for the restaurant's ever-changing menu. Now he's struck out on his own, opening Metrofresh—Good Food Fast, also in Atlanta. Metrofresh is a spot where Anderson put into action the enticing culinary secrets he learned at the heels of his favorite three cooks, his mother and two grandmothers.

THE SONGS: with the salad, *Bette Midler Sings Rosemary Clooney;* with dinner, *Andrea Boccelli* played softly, with dessert, *Chilled Out Music* Vols. 1 and 2

THE BEVERAGES: with the salad, 2 chilled flutes of Veuve Clicquot Champagne; with dinner, Rodney Strong Merlot; with dessert, coffee with Grand Marnier

Tuna Tartar with Mizuna Greens

NOTHING LIKE A LITTLE "RAW" FOOD TO GET THE BLOOD PUMPING AND THE PALATE SINGING! THIS RECIPE, AT FIRST READING, SEEMS HARDER TO PREPARE THAN IT REALLY IS. BE PATIENT. THE TARTAR AND THE DRESSING CAN BOTH BE PREPARED AHEAD OF TIME AND KEPT REFRIGERATED. IF YOU PREPARE THE CUCUMBERS AHEAD, STORE THEM SEPARATELY IN A TIGHTLY SEALED ZIPPERED BAG. THIS DISH ELEVATES SALAD TO ART. YOUR MAN WON'T FAIL TO BE IMPRESSED BY THE PRESENTATION.

FOR THE TARTAR:
3/4 pound sushi grade Ahi tuna, diced into 1/4-inch cubes (To properly dice the tuna, make sure you have a well-sharpened knife.)
1 small shallot, minced
1 tablespoon red onion, minced fine
1 teaspoon capers, rinsed and chopped
1 tablespoon Dijon mustard
1/4 cup rice wine vinegar
Salt and pepper to taste

Mix together the tuna, shallot, onion, capers, mustard, and vinegar in a medium-size, nonreactive bowl. Season with salt and pepper, and refrigerate.

FOR THE SALAD:
1/2 cup mizuna greens
1 small shallot, minced fine
1 teaspoon cumin powder, toasted (To toast the cumin, simply put it in a small skillet and heat over medium heat until the spice's flavor is notable. Do not burn.)
1/4 cup rice wine vinegar
1/2 cup extra-virgin olive oil
1 English (seedless) cucumber
1 cup cherry tomatoes, halved
Fresh, chopped chives for garnish

In a small bowl, mix the shallots, cumin, and vinegar. Gradually add the olive oil, whisking vigorously, until emulsified. Place the greens in a salad bowl, and toss gently with 1/2 of the dressing. Do not overdress! Meanwhile, using a peeler, remove several thin shavings of peeling and flesh from the cucumber. Place these shavings in a spring-loaded ring mold and center the mold on a large salad plate. Place 1/2 of the tartar in the bottom of the mold, pressing lightly to the edges, and top with the dressed mizuna. Carefully remove the ring mold, making sure the cucumber peelings remain upright and form a border around the salad and tartar. Repeat for the second salad, and garnish both with halved tomatoes and chopped chives.

MAKES 2 SERVINGS, WITH LEFTOVER DRESSING.

Beet Green Ravioli with Golden Beet Sauce and Red Beet Sticks

ANDERSON ADMITS THAT THIS SOUNDS LIKE BEET OVERKILL, BUT HE SAYS THERE IS SOMETHING DEEPLY SEDUCTIVE ABOUT THE FLAVOR OF GOLDEN AND RED BEETS TOGETHER. THE SAUCE FOR ANDERSON'S RAVIOLI IS AMAZINGLY RICH, WHILE THE PASTA ITSELF TASTES LIGHT AND DIVINE. PRETTY ON THE PLATE, THIS IS FOOD YOU'LL WANT TO NIBBLE ON WHILE YOU COOK. GO AHEAD AND SHARE A LITTLE PRE-MEAL SNACK OVER A SECOND GLASS OF CHAMPAGNE!

Beet greens from one bunch of beets, washed, trimmed, and de-stemmed (Swiss chard and chopped spinach both make wonderful substitutions for the beet greens.)
1 tablespoon extra-virgin olive oil
1 medium onion, chopped fine
2 cloves garlic, minced fine
$\frac{1}{2}$ cup ricotta cheese
$\frac{1}{2}$ cup Parmesan cheese, grated fine
Salt and pepper to taste
1 package wonton wrappers
2 eggs, beaten
$\frac{1}{4}$ teaspoon water
2 pounds golden beets, peeled and sliced
3 tablespoons butter

Bring a pot of water to a boil and add a generous amount of salt. Add the beet greens to the boiling water and cook until just tender. Fill a large mixing bowl with ice and top with water. When the greens are just tender, drain, then immediately transfer to the cold water bath to stop their cooking. After a minute or so in the cold water, drain the greens again, carefully wringing out all excess water using your hands; chop, and set aside in a mixing bowl. In a medium skillet, heat the olive oil and add the onion and garlic, sautéing until translucent. Do not brown. Remove the pan from heat. Once cooled, add the onion and garlic to the greens. Combine the ricotta and Parmesan, adding salt and pepper to taste. Add the cheese mixture to the greens and blend well to incorporate. Cover a baking sheet with waxed paper and lightly flour the paper. Lay out the wonton squares on a clean surface. Add the water to the beaten eggs and stir well. Brush the egg wash over the wontons and place a small amount of the beet green–cheese mixture in the middle of each square. Fold the wonton over, forming a triangle, and press around the edges to seal, first with your fingers, then with the tines of a fork. Place the sealed ravioli on the baking sheet and refrigerate until ready to use. Meanwhile, fill a large saucepan with enough water to cover the beets, and add the butter. Bring to a boil and cook the beets until very tender and the water has reduced significantly. Once soft, remove the beets from the water and place them in a blender or food processor. Puree until smooth, add salt and pepper to taste, and return the puree to the empty saucepan and keep warm. Fill a large pasta pot with water, add a generous dose of salt, and bring to a boil. Add the ravioli, one by one, using a slotted spoon, and cook for approximately 7 minutes or until soft. Place 1/2 cup of beet puree on each dinner plate and spread to cover using a wooden spoon. Top with the ravioli, artfully arranged, and garnish with the beet sticks (recipe follows).

MAKES 2 SERVINGS.

Beet Sticks

FESTIVE TO THE EYE AND OH-SO-DELICIOUS, YOU'LL HAVE TO MUSTER PLENTY OF WILLPOWER TO RESIST MUNCHING ON THESE SALTY DELIGHTS BEFORE SERVING.

4 to 5 large beets, peeled and cut into matchsticks
2 cups fine flour, preferably Wondra brand
3½ quarts canola oil
Salt to taste

Place the beet sticks in a colander and lightly shake the flour over them, tossing to coat well. Allow the flour to dry on the beets for approximately 10 minutes. Heat the oil in an 8-quart saucepan or a deep fryer until it reaches 350 to 375 degrees F. Gently toss the beet sticks in the oil a small handful at a time. The oil will splatter. Stir occasionally once the oil has ceased to splatter, and cook until crispy, approximately 3 to 4 minutes. Remove with a slotted spoon and drain on a paper towel. Salt the beet sticks lightly while still warm. Before frying the next handful of beets, be sure that the oil has returned to 350 degrees F.

MAKES 2 SERVINGS.

Häagen-Dazs Mango Ice Cream with Fried Bananas and Raspberry Sauce

THIS IS ANDERSON'S NO-FAIL RECIPE FOR SUCCESS WITH YOUR MAN. A TROPICAL SENSATION, IT SETS THE STAGE FOR AN EVENING IN PARADISE.

2 10-ounce packages frozen raspberries
½ cup sugar
2 tablespoons corn starch
¼ cup water
½ cup Chambord liqueur
2 ripe bananas
2 tablespoons canola oil
1 pint Häagen-Dazs mango ice cream

Combine the raspberries, sugar, corn starch, water, and Chambord in a small saucepan and bring to a boil. Reduce the heat to a simmer and stir occasionally, cooking until the mixture thickens to a dense syrup. Place a strainer over a small bowl and pour the sauce through it, working with a wooden spoon to squeeze the sauce from the raspberries. You will have about 2 cups sauce. Refrigerate until ready to serve. Slice the bananas in half lengthwise. Heat the oil in a skillet and add the bananas, frying for approximately 1 to 2 minutes per side. The bananas should be soft and slightly browned. Place 2 scoops of ice cream on a small plate. Arrange the bananas over the ice cream, teepee style, and drizzle raspberry sauce over the top.

MAKES 2 SERVINGS.

Chapter 27
John Woodruff

This man is all about life in the fast lane.

Woodruff's ancestors founded the Coca-Cola Company—an all-American corporate powerhouse if there ever was one—and you could swear that he was born with caffeine in his bloodstream. An energy-driven racecar enthusiast and helicopter pilot, Woodruff also enjoys the adrenaline kick he gets behind the wheel of his 100-mph, turbine-powered racing boat. When he's not thrilling in the power of jet fuel, Woodruff spends time getting his children to school and cruising the open roads, family in tow, in his luxury, 45-foot Prevost tour bus. This menu is his favorite for a comfortable night at home, complete with a classic family dessert topped with a bright little cherry.

THE SONG: *Against All Odds* by Phil Collins

THE BEVERAGE: A mixed drink of his choice followed by a nice bottle of Shiraz

Stuffed Celery and Assorted Crudités for Dipping

SIMPLE PLEASURES APPEAL TO THIS HIGH-LIVING MAN. HE LOVES TO DUNK HIS VEGGIES IN A THICK, CREAMY BLUE CHEESE OR RANCH DIP AND ENGAGE IN LIGHT, PRE-DINNER CONVERSATION.

6 celery ribs, peeled to remove strings
1 package cream cheese
1 cup sour cream
1 cup mayonnaise, preferably Hellmann's
6 ounces blue cheese, crumbled
$\frac{1}{2}$ teaspoon white pepper
1 package baby carrots
1 red bell pepper, sliced thin
1 head of broccoli, cut into florets

Slice the celery on the diagonal into 3-inch lengths. Spread cream cheese into the hollow of each celery stick, and arrange on a relish plate. In a small bowl, combine the sour cream and mayonnaise until well blended. Add the cheese, mixing well to combine. Season with pepper and serve alongside baby carrots, bell pepper, and broccoli florets.

MAKES 2-4 SERVINGS.

Baked Chicken Tenderloin in a Curry Cream Sauce

ANOTHER MEAL-MADE-SIMPLE, THIS IS JOHN WOODRUFF'S ALL-PURPOSE RECIPE FOR A SIMPLE, TASTY ENTREE THAT PAIRS WELL WITH A SIDE OF BABY SWEET PEAS, A MOUND OF WHITE RICE, AND SOME SLICED PEAR. THIS COMES TOGETHER QUICKLY AND SHOULD BE PREPARED BEFORE YOUR MAN DARKENS THE DOOR. HE'LL NO DOUBT ASK ABOUT THE RECIPE—KEEP THE INGREDIENTS TOP SECRET. MEN LOVE MYSTERY.

2 boneless, skinless chicken breasts
1 tablespoon extra-virgin olive oil
2 celery ribs, peeled to remove strings, and chopped
1 12-ounce can cream of celery soup
1 12-ounce can golden mushroom soup
1 12-ounce can water
1 tablespoon Worcestershire sauce
1 tablespoon curry powder
1 teaspoon garlic powder
Freshly ground pepper

Preheat the oven to 300 degrees F. Wash chicken breasts and pat dry. Place them in a glass baking dish and set aside. In a medium skillet, heat the olive oil over high heat and add the celery, sautéing until soft. Lower the heat and add the celery and mushroom soups and water. Stir to combine and warm thoroughly. Add the Worcestershire sauce, curry powder, garlic powder, and freshly ground black pepper and stir well. Remove from heat and pour over the chicken breasts. Bake, covered, for approximately one hour, or until the juices of the chicken breast run clear when pricked with a fork. Serve with white rice, baby peas, and sliced pear.

MAKES 2 SERVINGS.

Classic Coca-Cola Cake

THIS IS AN OLD-TIME FAVORITE THAT WOODRUFF CAN'T RESIST. BAKING IT WILL BRING OUT THE CHILD IN YOU. KEEP THE MOOD PLAYFUL AS YOU SHARE A SLICE WITH YOUR MAN.

FOR THE CAKE:
2 cups sugar
2 cups unbleached flour
$\frac{1}{2}$ cup butter
3 tablespoons cocoa powder
$\frac{1}{2}$ cup vegetable oil
1 cup Coca-Cola Classic
$\frac{1}{2}$ cup buttermilk
1 teaspoon baking soda
2 large eggs, well beaten
1 teaspoon vanilla extract
1$\frac{1}{2}$ cups miniature marshmallows

FOR THE FROSTING:
$\frac{1}{2}$ cup margarine
3 tablespoons cocoa powder
6 tablespoons Coca-Cola Classic
1 pound powdered sugar
1 cup pecans, chopped
Maraschino cherries for garnish

Preheat the oven to 350 degrees F. Grease and flour a 13-x-9-inch cake pan. Over a large bowl, sift together the sugar and flour. In a heavy saucepan, mix the butter, cocoa, oil, and Coca-Cola, and bring to a boil over high heat. Pour this mixture over the dry ingredients, blending well. Stir in the buttermilk, baking soda, vanilla, eggs, and marshmallows, blending well. Do not beat this mixture. Pour into the cake pan and bake for 45 minutes, or until a toothpick inserted in the center of the cake comes out clean. Allow to cool for at least 30 minutes before frosting. Meanwhile, for the frosting, bring the margarine, cocoa powder and Coke to a boil for one minute in a small saucepan. Remove from heat and gradually add the sugar. Stir in the pecans and allow to cool. Spread frosting across the top of the cake and add cherries for garnish.

MAKES 6 SERVINGS.

Chapter 28
Martin Yan

It's one of the most seductive traits a mate can possess—wit—and Chef Martin Yan has built his reputation on it. This TV chef extraordinaire has wooed budding chefs with his easy-to-prepare Asian fare as host of more than 2,000 cooking shows broadcast worldwide, and he's still found the time to share his expertise in print, too, counting 26 cookbook titles to his name. Obviously, Chef Yan is no stranger to love in the kitchen. This Chinese-born Master Chef began his formal training at age 13. Today he owns a namesake cooking school and two successful Pan-Asian restaurants as well. With this spirited menu, Chef Yan presents his trademark talent, ensuring you and yours an exotic evening of fun.

THE SONG: *Your Song* by Elton John

THE BEVERAGE: Passion Fruit Bellini (recipe follows)

Passion Fruit Bellini

YAN'S TROPICAL TAKE ON THE CLASSIC PEACH-FLAVORED FAVORITE IS DIVINE. ONE SIP, AND YOU CAN FEEL THE WHITE SANDS AND AZURE WATERS UNDERFOOT. TWO SIPS, AND YOUR MAN WILL BE FAWNING OVER YOU AS IF YOU WERE ALONE ON A DESERTED ISLAND. MMMM . . .

8 ounces passion fruit juice
½ bottle sparkling wine or champagne, brut

Chill both the juice and sparkling wine prior to mixing the drink. In each of two chilled champagne flutes, pour about 1/2 cup of passion fruit juice, or enough to fill the glass about 1/3 full. Fill the remaining 2/3 of each glass with sparkling wine, and serve.

MAKES 2 SERVINGS.

Flower Petal Dumplings*

DELICIOUS GEMS SURE TO GET YOUR EVENING OFF ON THE RIGHT FOOT, YAN'S DUMPLINGS ARE THE PERFECT PALATE-TEASERS WITH THEIR MIX OF CHICKEN AND PORK JAZZED UP BY FRESH GINGER AND GREEN ONIONS. THEY LOOK (AND TASTE!) AS THOUGH THEY'D BE IMPOSSIBLY TIME-CONSUMING TO PREPARE, BUT THEY'RE ACTUALLY READY IN A SNAP. FIRST TIME IS A CHARM, BUT YOU'LL RETURN TO THIS RECIPE AGAIN AND AGAIN WHEN IT COMES TO SNAGGING THAT MAN!

2 dried black mushrooms
¼ pound napa cabbage, chopped fine
¼ pound lean ground chicken
¼ pound lean ground pork
1 tablespoon green onions, chopped
2 teaspoons minced ginger
2 tablespoons oyster-flavored sauce
1 teaspoon sesame oil
¼ teaspoon white pepper

*From www.yancancook.com, Yan Can Cook, Inc., 2005

18 gyoza or potsticker wrappers
2 tablespoons frozen peas, thawed
3 tablespoons cooking oil
²/₃ cup chicken broth
Soy sauce, chili oil, and rice vinegar for dipping

Prepare filling: Soak mushrooms in warm water to cover until softened, about 20 minutes; drain. Trim and discard stems. Finely chop caps. Place cabbage in a clean towel and squeeze to remove excess water. Combine mushrooms and cabbage in a bowl and add remaining filling ingredients; mix well. To fill each dumpling, place a heaping teaspoon of filling in center of a wrapper; keep remaining wrappers covered to prevent drying. Fold wrapper in half to form a semi-circle; pinch center to seal. Bring opposite sides of wrapper together and pinch to seal so the top starts to form petals. Line up edges and pinch to seal. Place a pea on top for garnish. Cover filled dumplings with a dry towel. Place a wide frying pan over medium heat until hot. Add 1½ tablespoons cooking oil, swirling to coat sides. Add dumplings, half at a time, seam side up. Cook until bottoms are golden brown, 3 to 4 minutes. Add 1/3 cup broth; reduce heat to low, cover, and cook until liquid is absorbed, 5 to 6 minutes. Place dumplings on a serving plate with soy sauce, chili oil, and vinegar on the side.

MAKES 18 DUMPLINGS.

Seared Sea Scallops in Sweet Chili Sauce*

SCALLOPS ARE BELIEVED BY MANY TO BE AN APHRODISIAC. THIS RECIPE SERVES UP A DOUBLE WHAMMY WITH THE SCALLOPS' FLIRTATIOUS SWEET CHILI SAUCE AS A FOIL FOR THE SHELLFISH. SUPER EASY TO PREPARE AND SUPER PLEASING TO EAT, YAN PROVES THAT PULLING OUT ALL THE STOPS DOESN'T HAVE TO BE DIFFICULT.

MARINADE
2 tablespoons fresh lime juice
1 tablespoon fish sauce
1 teaspoon grated ginger

½ pound sea scallops

1 tablespoon vegetable oil

*From www.yancancook.com, Yan Can Cook, Inc., 2005

3 tablespoons sweet chili sauce
1 tablespoon chicken broth
1 teaspoon chili garlic sauce

Hot steamed rice
2 tablespoons chopped cilantro

Combine marinade ingredients in a medium bowl. Add scallops and stir to coat.
Let stand for 10 minutes. Drain scallops and pat dry with paper towels. Heat a wide
frying pan over medium-high heat until hot. Add oil, swirling to coat the bottom.
When oil is hot, add scallops and pan-fry, turning once, until golden brown, about
2 minutes on each side. Combine sweet chili sauce, broth, and chili garlic sauce
in a small saucepan; heat to simmering. Simmer until sauce thickens slightly, about
2 minutes. Serve scallops with rice, drizzle with sauce, and garnish with cilantro.

MAKES 2 SERVINGS.

Five-Spice Pineapple Banana Split for Two*

AN ASIAN TWIST ON AN ICE-CREAM PARLOR CLASSIC, CHEF YAN SPICES THINGS UP WITH ARO-
MATIC CHINESE FIVE-SPICE POWDER. A SPICE TYPICALLY USED IN SAVORY COOKING, CHINESE
FIVE-SPICE SENDS THIS PINEAPPLE-TOPPED BANANA SPLIT COMPLETELY OVER THE TOP.

PINEAPPLE TOPPING
4-ounce can crushed pineapple, undrained
2 tablespoons water
2 teaspoons dark brown sugar
$1/2$ teaspoon grated ginger
$1/4$ teaspoon Chinese five-spice powder

1 ripe banana, peeled and halved lengthwise
2 large scoops vanilla or coconut ice cream
Purchased chocolate syrup
Whipped cream
$1/4$ cup purchased glazed walnuts

*From www.yancancook.com, Yan Can Cook, Inc., 2005

Combine pineapple topping ingredients in a small saucepan. Cook over medium heat, stirring occasionally, until sugar dissolves and syrup thickens slightly, about 5 minutes. Assemble dessert: arrange bananas, cut side up, in an oval dessert dish. Top bananas with ice cream, warm pineapple topping, a few tablespoons of the chocolate, and a dollop of whipped cream. Sprinkle glazed walnuts over the top and serve with two spoons.

MAKES 2 SERVINGS.

Chapter 29
Charles Gargano

Nobody says I love New York better than Charles Gargano. As chairman and CEO of Empire State Development and an assistant to the New York City mayor, Gargano oversees billions of dollars daily as he heads up the Big Apple's post-9/11 economic recovery efforts and the redevelopment of Lower Manhattan. This man may have invented the power lunch—wining and dining his way through the nation's leading city for culturally diverse food is all in a day's work for him.

THE SONG: *Strangers in the Night* by Frank Sinatra

THE BEVERAGE: Gianni Gagliardo Barolo Preve, Italy

Tomato, Mozzarella di Bufala, and Basil Salad

GARGANO KNOWS THAT THE THREE COLORS OF THIS SPIRITED SALAD REPRESENT THE COLORS OF ITALY'S NATIONAL FLAG, AND HE BETS THIS SALAD'S BOLD FLAVOR WILL IGNITE YOUR MAN'S INNER ITALIAN! SAY *BUON GIORNO* TO YOUR HOT, NEW ITALIAN LOVER.

2 large beefsteak tomatoes, sliced ¼-inch thick
2 balls fresh buffalo mozzarella, sliced ¼-inch thick
12 fresh basil leaves
4 tablespoons good quality extra-virgin olive oil
4 tablespoons balsamic vinegar
Freshly ground black pepper
Sea salt

Arrange the sliced tomatoes and mozzarella in alternating and overlapping fashion on two large dinner plates. Decorate with the fresh basil leaves, slightly tucking them in between the tomatoes and cheese. Drizzle with the olive oil and balsamic vinegar and sprinkle with sea salt and pepper to taste.

MAKES 2 SERVINGS.

Veal Chops Milanese

PERFECT LIGHT DINING THAT IS LONG ON FLAVOR, VEAL CHOPS MILANESE IS ANOTHER ITALIAN-STYLE FAVORITE OF GARGANO'S. THIS IS TRATTORIA FARE AT ITS BEST. ENJOY IT AL FRESCO IF THE WEATHER ALLOWS.

2 veal rib chops on the bone
1 egg, beaten
Salt
Freshly ground black pepper
1 cup plain bread crumbs
2 tablespoons olive oil
¼ cup clarified butter (see Note, p. 32)
1 cup arugula leaves
½ cup fresh tomato, diced into ½-inch cubes

¼ cup imported Italian Parmesan-Reggiano, shaved
1 lemon, halved with seeds removed

Trim any gristle and fat from the veal chop and cut the meat away from the bone slightly, leaving the bone attached. Cover the chop with plastic wrap and pound the meat until it is approximately 1/8-inch thick all over. Season the beaten egg with salt and pepper. Place the bread crumbs in a large, flat plate. Dip each chop into the egg mixture and then into the bread crumbs, patting the crumbs to help them stick to each side of the meat. In a large skillet or sauté pan large enough to hold both veal chops side-by-side, heat the olive oil and clarified butter over high heat. Add the chops, reduce the heat to medium, and cook until the bread crumbs turn golden. Flip and cook on the other side, careful not to overcook the veal. Maximum cooking time per side is 6 minutes; less for a thinner chop. Arrange each chop in the center of a dinner plate. Top each with fresh arugula leaves followed by diced tomatoes. Top with the shaved parmesan and lemon wedges and serve immediately.

MAKES 2 SERVINGS.

Grapefruit Sorbet with Fresh Berries

A SPOONFUL OF TARTNESS TAMED BY THE SWEETNESS OF BERRIES, SORBET IS A REFRESHING WAY TO END YOUR MEAL. THE GRAPEFRUIT WILL GIVE YOU BOTH A CITRUS KICK—AN INVIGORATING FINISH TO PUT YOU IN THE STARTING BLOCKS FOR WHAT'S TO COME.

2 cups sugar
4 cups water
2 cups freshly squeezed grapefruit juice
1 cup mixed, fresh, seasonal berries, such as blueberries, raspberries and
    strawberries
2 sprigs fresh mint

Combine the sugar and water in a small saucepan and bring to a boil. Add the grapefruit juice, remove from heat, and allow to cool. Chill thoroughly. Pour the chilled mixture into the container of an electric or hand-cranked ice cream freezer, and freeze, according to manufacturer's instructions. Place 2 scoops of frozen sorbet in a chilled parfait or wine glass. Top with the mixed berries and garnish with mint.

MAKES 2 SERVINGS.

Index